Class Piano Resource Materials

Level Four

(Fifth Edition)

Compiled and edited by
W. Daniel Landes

© 2006, 2011 by Smith Creek Music
PO Box 140449, Nashville, TN 37214
www.smithcreekmusic.com

Class Piano Resource Materials
Level Four
(Fifth Edition)

© 2006, 2011 by Smith Creek Music
PO Box 140446
Nashville, TN 37214

www.smithcreekmusic.com
E-mail: info@smithcreekmusic.com

All rights reserved.

ISBN: 978-0-9835362-4-6

Except as otherwise stated, all rights on all material are reserved by Smith Creek Music. No part of this collection may be reproduced or transmitted in any form or by any means, electronic or mechanical, including photocopying, recording, or by any information storage or retrieval system, except as may be expressly permitted by the 1976 Copyright Act or in writing from the publisher.

Other Class Piano Resource Materials are available from Smith Creek Music, PO Box 140446, Nashville, TN 37214
Please e-mail us at info@smithcreekmusic.com or visit our WEB site at www.smithcreekmusic.com for ordering information.

Introduction

These ***Class Piano Resource Materials*** were compiled for use in the secondary piano program at Belmont University, Nashville, TN. Consequently, the content has been shaped to a large extent by the various degree programs at that school and in particular, the Piano Proficiency Examination. Every school/department of music has some type of piano proficiency evaluation that music majors must pass in order to complete their degree requirements. The various parts of the proficiency examination are the basic piano skills: repertory, scales and arpeggios, chords, harmonizing melodies, improvisation, transposition, etc. Consequently, the ***Class Piano Resource Materials*** are designed to prepare the student to pass a piano proficiency examination. Although intended for use in college classes, the materials are broad enough to be used in any class piano setting where there is a need for a graded series of books with a broad range of musical styles.

SCOPE OF THE MATERIALS

The ***Class Piano Resource Materials*** are arranged in five books by level of difficulty: Preparatory Level (no prior keyboard experience is assumed), Level One, Level Two, Level Three, and Level Four. Each level is organized according to specific goals that are spelled out clearly at the beginning of the book. Theory skills are not addressed in great detail because it is assumed that secondary piano classes are required in conjunction with the various theory classes such as Fundamentals of Music, Harmony, and Form. Detailed pedagogical information is outside the scope of these ***Resource Materials*** because it is believed that the instructor will give the necessary explanation of such things as keyboard technique, fingering, and style. Nevertheless, all the books in the various levels are organized in an increasing level of difficulty if the instructor chooses to use them in that way. In addition, a suggested assignment schedule based on a 15-week semester is included in each level to aid the instructor in preparing weekly lesson plans.

DESCRIPTION OF THE MATERIALS

In selecting the materials, specific composers and periods of music were a strong factor. Each level contains representative repertory by classical composers such as Bach and Beethoven. Twentieth century classical music composers such as Bartók, Persichetti, and Schoenberg are included as well as representative pieces in various styles composed specifically for these books by the author. Each level includes music in a popular style. These are not arrangements of popular tunes but are original compositions which appear here for the first time. It is hoped that the choice of repertory and other material will give the student a well-rounded musical experience and help develop keyboard and musicianship skills necessary for the professional musician.

INTEGRATION OF TECHNOLOGY

Each book has an accompanying interactive computer application that been designed as an additional resource, including links to a WEB site. The application runs on Apple Macintosh computers using system OSX 10.2 and higher. Versions for Windows computers, IPads, and other electronic devices may be available in the future. Detailed information regarding the implementation of the computer applications is available on the website:

www.smithcreekmusic.com

COPYRIGHTS

Every effort has been made to contact the owners of copyrights for permission to make settings or use pieces. If mistakes have occurred, they will be corrected as soon as possible. Please email us at:

info@smithcreekmusic.com.

The author is grateful to the owners of copyrighted material who have granted permission to use their works. Where copyrighted material is used, a copyright notice appears at the bottom of the page.

Table of Contents

                                                Page

Introduction	iii
Goals for Level Four	vi
Class Notes	vii

REPERTORY

The Primrose (Peerson)	8
Minuet in F (Mozart)	10
Scotch Dance (Beethoven)	11
Solfeggietto (Bach)	12
Bagatelle (Beethoven)	15
Minuet in G (Bach)	16
Sonatina (Clementi)	18
Tableaux No. 1: Pleading (Rebikov)	20
Prelude in C Minor (Chopin)	22
Peacherine Rag (Joplin)	23
A Valse for Vivian (Baker)	24
Belmont Boogie (Landes)	26
Sarabande (Handel)	28
To a Wild Rose (MacDowell)	30
Uncle Willie Rides Off into the Sunset (Landes)	32
Debbie Reflects on the Indiscretions of Her Youth (Landes)	34

FOUR-PART CHORALES, HYMNS AND PATRIOTIC SONGS

America: My Country, 'tis of Thee (anon.)	36
Materna: America the Beautiful (Ward)	37
National Anthem: The Star-Spangled Banner (Smith)	38
Old 100th (tune by Bourgeois; arr. anon)	40
Nicaea (Dykes)	41
Passion Chorale (Bach)	42
St. Theodulph (Teschner/Monk)	43
Azmon (Mason)	44
Canonbury (Schumann)	44
Crusader's Hymn (anon.)	45
St. Anne (Croft/Monk)	45
Hymn to Joy (Beethoven/Hodges)	46
Nun Danket Alle Gott (Crüger/Mendelssohn)	47

	Page
Root Positions Triads	48
Procedures for Harmonizing Melodies	52
Block-Chord Cadences	54
Accompaniment Patterns	58
Melodies for Harmonization	60
Improvisation	74
Sight Reading and Transposition I: Piano Scores	82
Sight Reading and Transposition II: Open Scores	96
Scales: Explanation of Groups and Characteristics	112
Scales in Notation Arranged by Group	114
Arpeggios	123
Scale and Arpeggio Practice log	129
Exercises	130
Class Notes	137

APPENDIXES

Appendix 1: Triads in a Scale; Inversions of Triads	144
Appendix 2: Melodic Phrases	149
Appendix 3: Melodic Cadences	150
Appendix 4: Non-Chord Tone	152
Weekly Assignment Schedule	154
Class Notes	158
Level Four Assignment Chart	159

For more resources, please visit the WEB SITE at:

www.smithcreekmusic.com

General Goals
(Level Four)

1. Reinforce orientation to the keyboard:

    -- demonstrate an understanding of proper sitting position and hand position
    -- play in the correct octave
    -- demonstrate an understanding of basic hand positions: 5-finger hand positions, octave hand positions

2. Play major, natural minor, and harmonic minor scales in Group I and II; play major and harmonic minor scales in Group III. Play Group II melodic minor scales in these keys: Cm, Dm, Em, Gm, and Am. See explanation in the scale section of this volume.

3. Play assigned repertory pieces with acceptable proficiency.

4. Demonstrate an understanding of the proper use of the sustain pedal.

5. Play root position major, minor, augmented and diminished triads on any note.

6. Play block-style cadences in major and minor keys through two accidentals.

7. Play pieces in a 4-part setting (chorales, hymns).

8. Harmonize melodies using primary chords and secondary dominants.

9. Improvise simple melodies (chord tones, passing tones, neighbor tones) over given chord progressions in major and minor keys through two accidentals.

10. Create simple improvised arrangements of familiar melodies.

11. Transpose a single line (treble or bass clef) up and down a half step and whole step.

12. Using the Cadence #1 progression, establish all major and minor keys.

13. Demonstrate sight reading proficiency.

14. Play simple technical exercises.

15. Continue to develop concepts of style and musicianship and demonstrate these in the performance of assigned repertory:

    -- expression
    -- articulation
    -- dynamics
    -- tempo

16. Pass the Piano Proficiency Examination.

Class Notes

The Primrose

Martin Peerson
c. 1600

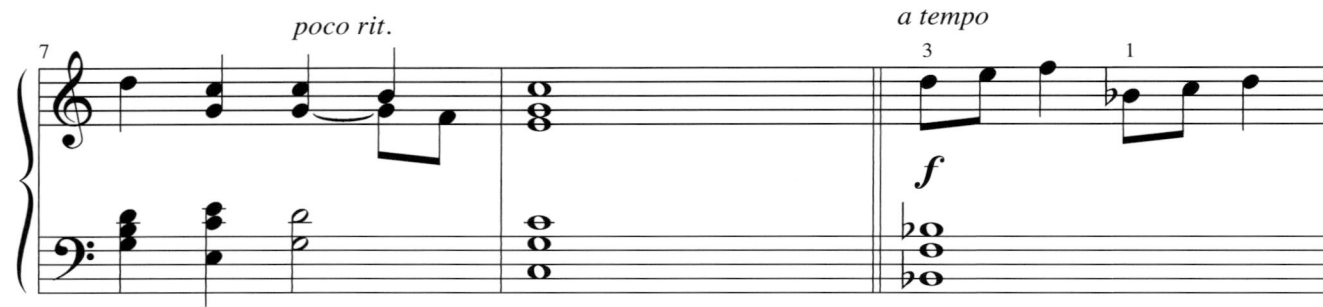

Music © 2001 by Smith Creek Music, Nashville, TN 37214. All rights reserved. www.smithcreekmusic.com

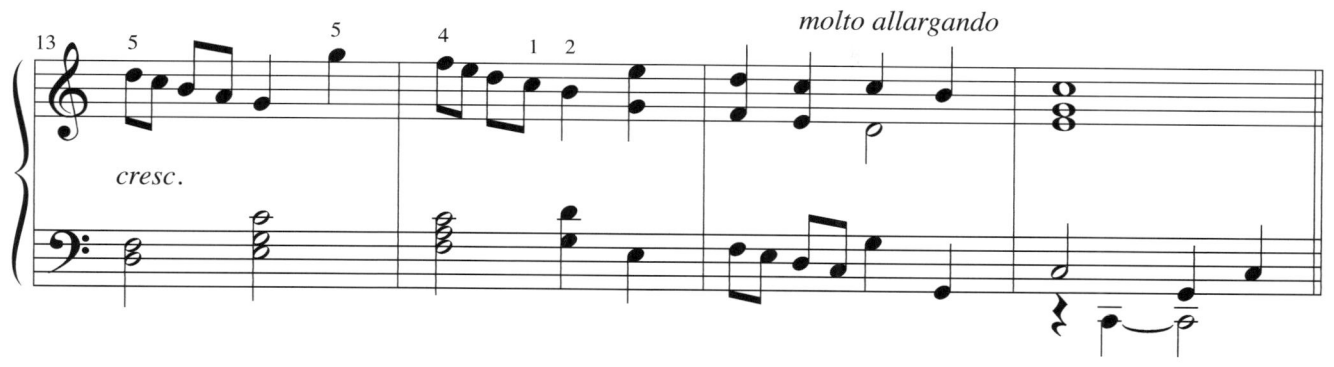

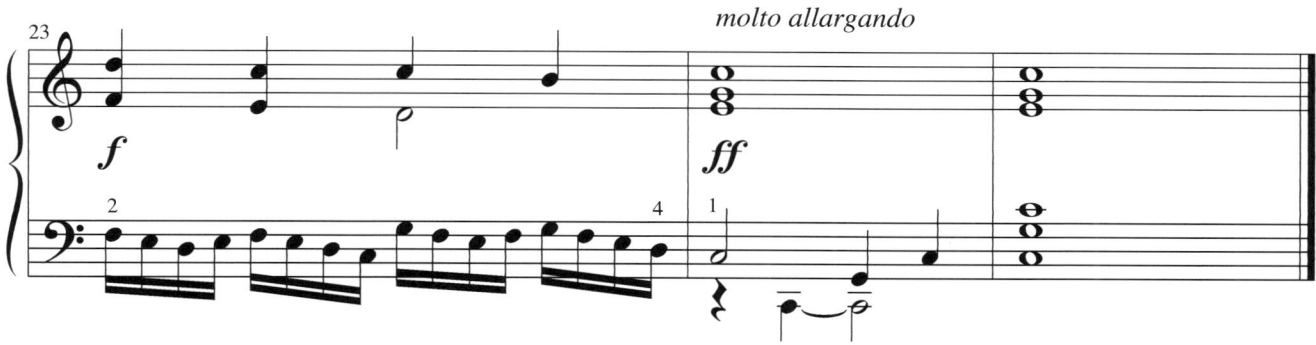

Minuet

W. A. Mozart

Scotch Dance

L. van Beethoven

Solfeggietto

C. P. E. Bach, ca 1760

Bagatelle

Ludwig van Beethoven

Minuet in G

From the Notebook of Anna Magdalena Bach

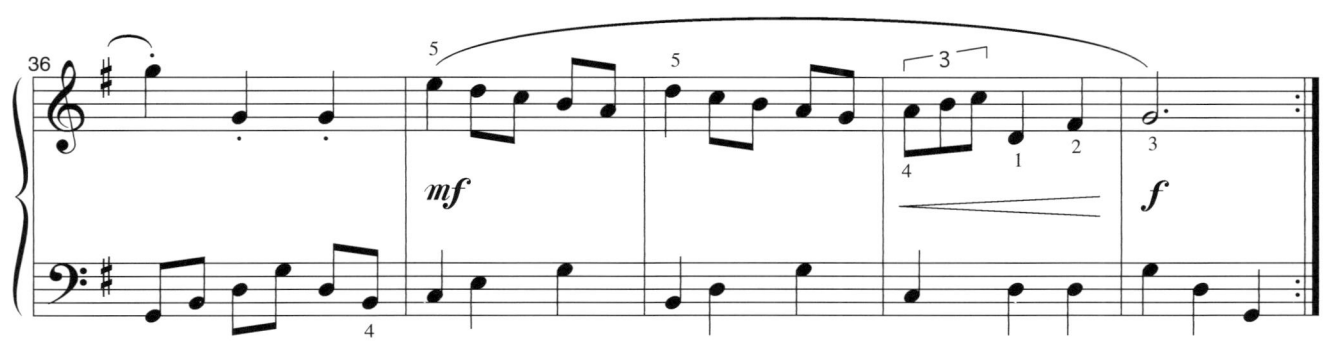

17

Sonatina

Muzio Clementi

Tableaux No. 3: Ancient Worlds

Vladimir Rebikov
arr. WDL

Prelude in C Minor

Frederick Chopin

Peacherine Rag

Scott Joplin

Valse for Vivian

Buddy Baker and David Hanson
Adapted for piano solo by WDL

Original music copyright © 1982 by Studio P/R, Hialeah, Fla. Used by permission.
Arrangement copyright © 2011 by Smith Creek Music, Nashville, TN. All Rights Reserved. www.smithcreekmusic.com

Belmont Boogie

Any tempo that feels good

WDL

Music © 2001 by Smith Creek Music, Nashville, TN 37214. All rights reserved. www.smithcreekmusic.com

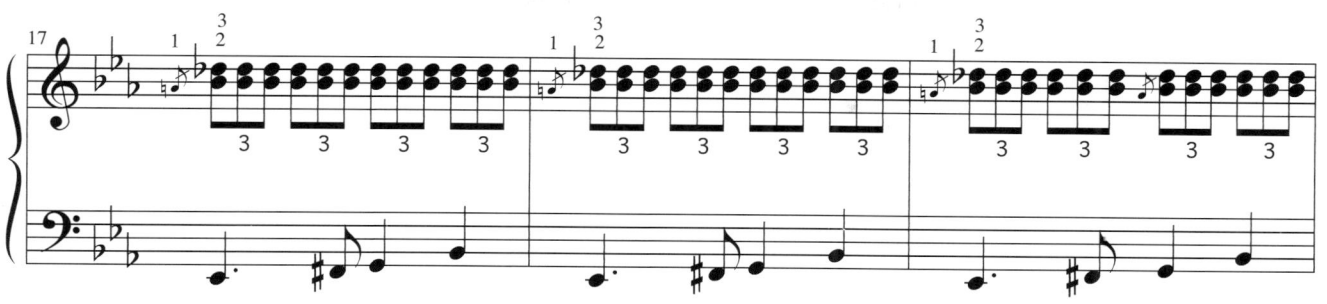
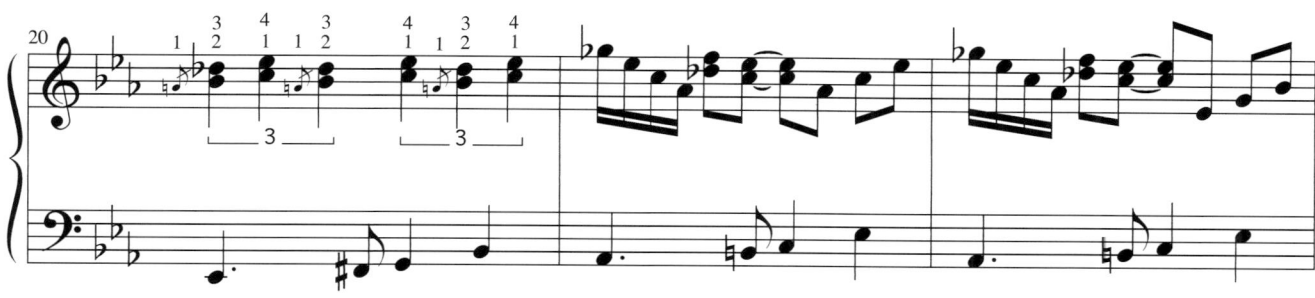

27

Sarabande

G. F. Handel
arr. WDL

The original version of this piece had no written dynamics. Try adding your own.

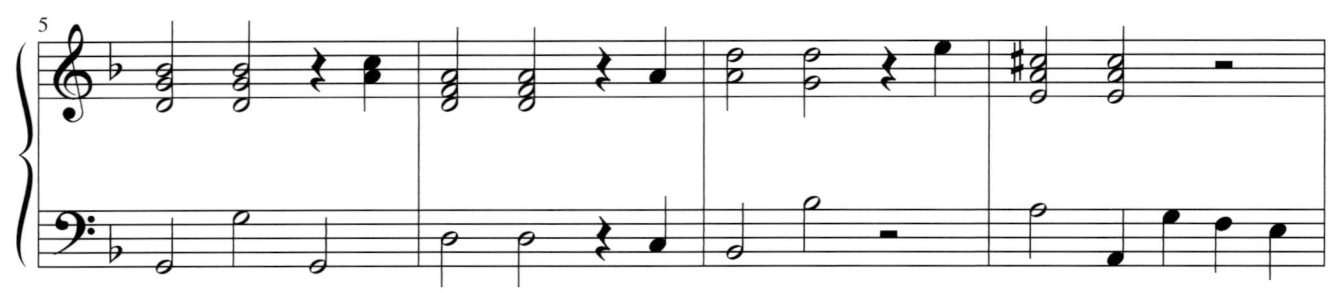

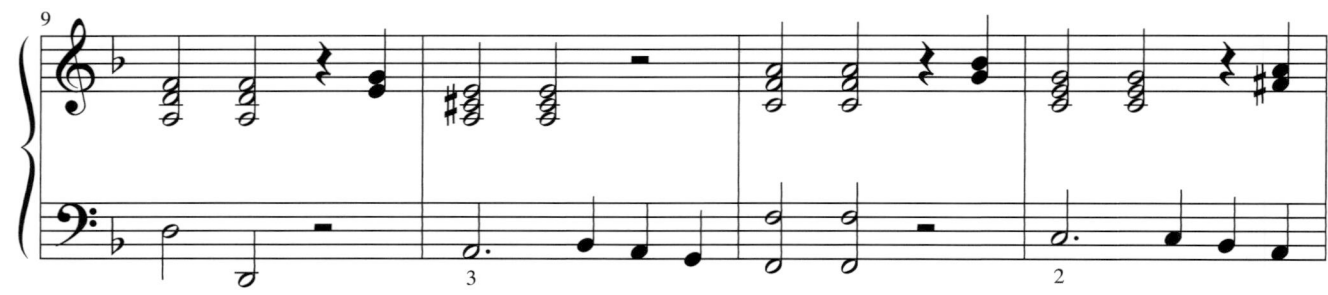

Music © 2001 by Smith Creek Music, Nashville, TN 37214. All rights reserved. www.smithcreekmusic.com

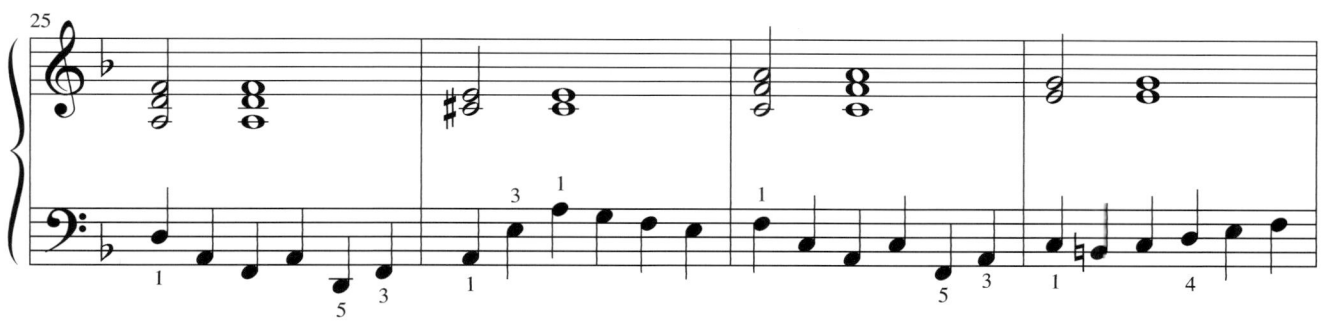
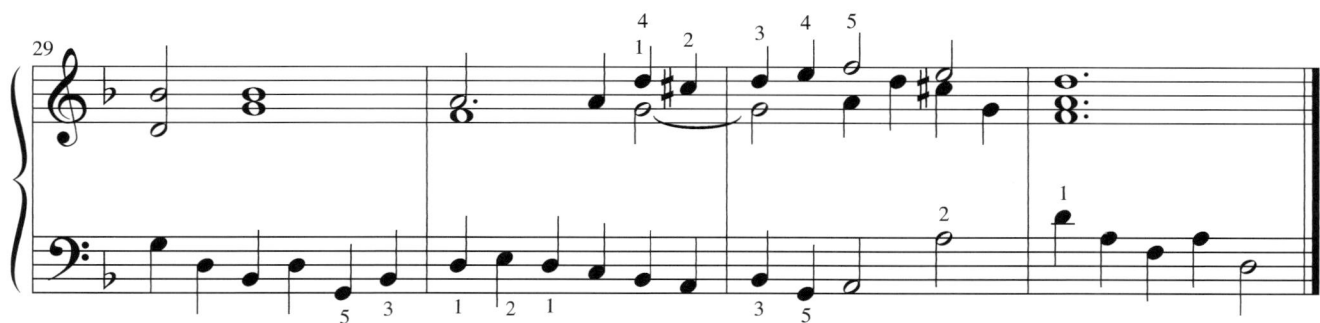

Based on the original version published ca. 1732

To a Wild Rose

Edward MacDowell
arr. by WDL

Moderato

* use sustain pedal

Music © 2011 by Smith Creek Music, Nashville, TN 37214. All rights reserved. www.smithcreekmusic.com

Uncle Willie Rides Off into the Sunset

WDL

Debbie Reflects on the Indiscretions of Her Youth

My Country, 'Tis of Thee

AMERICA
from *Thesaurus Musicus*, 1744

* Play the tenor note (d) with the right hand.

America, The Beautiful

MATERNA
Samuel Ward, c. 1885

The Star-Spangled Banner

NATIONAL ANTHEM
John Stanford Smith, ca. 1765

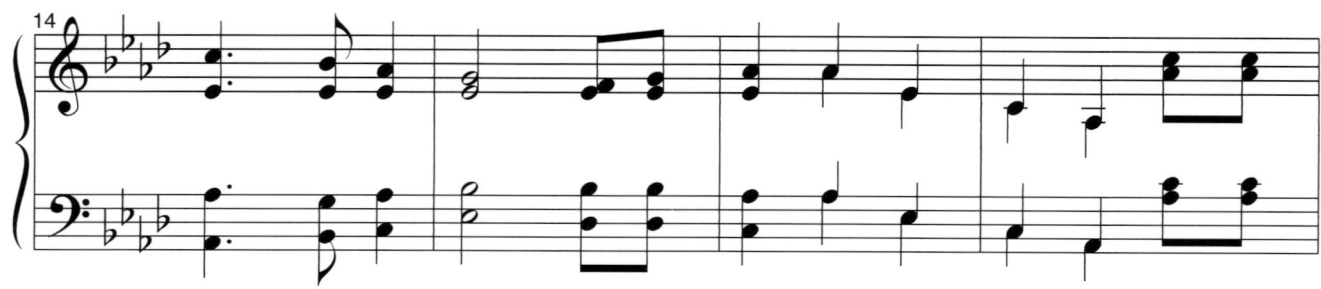

The "Star-Spangled Banner," lyrics by Francis Scott Key (1814), was adopted as the National Anthem of the United States of America by an act of Congress in 1931.

Old 100th

OLD 100th
tune by Louis Bourgeois, 1551

(Isorhythmic version)

(Rhythmic version)

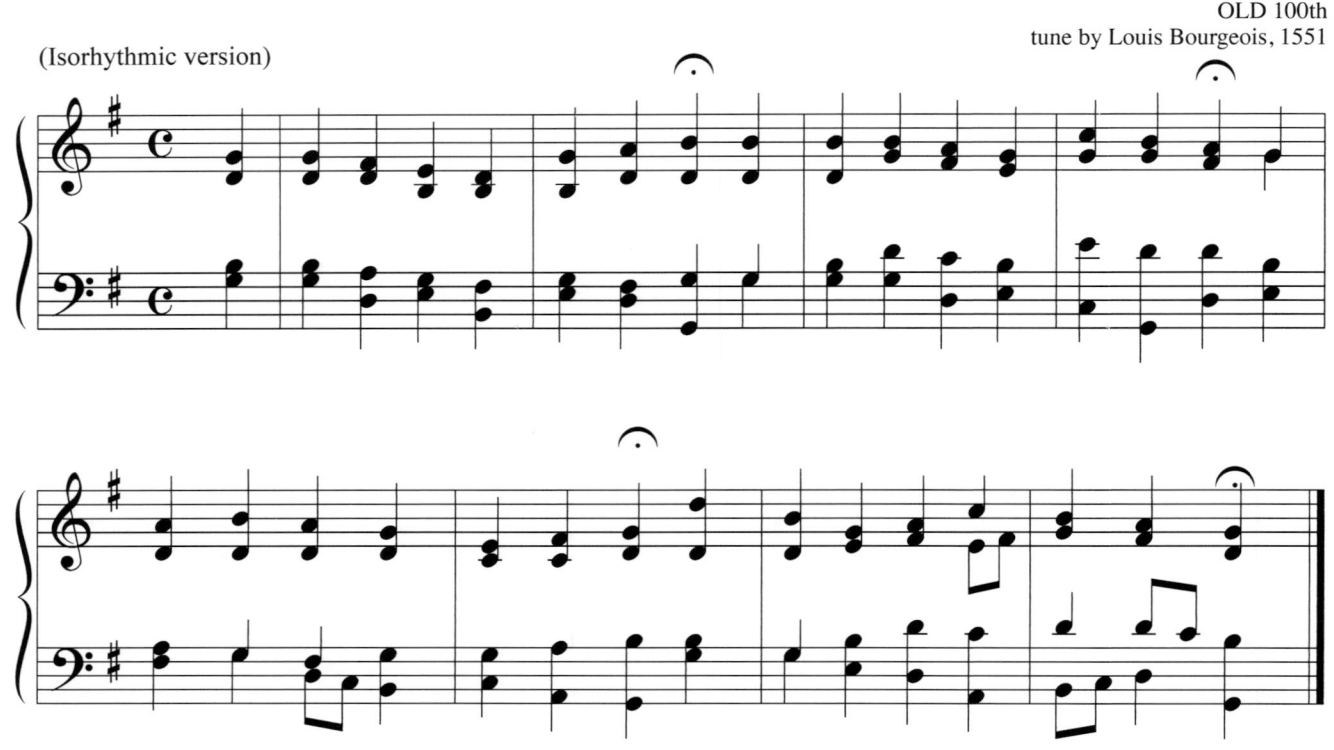

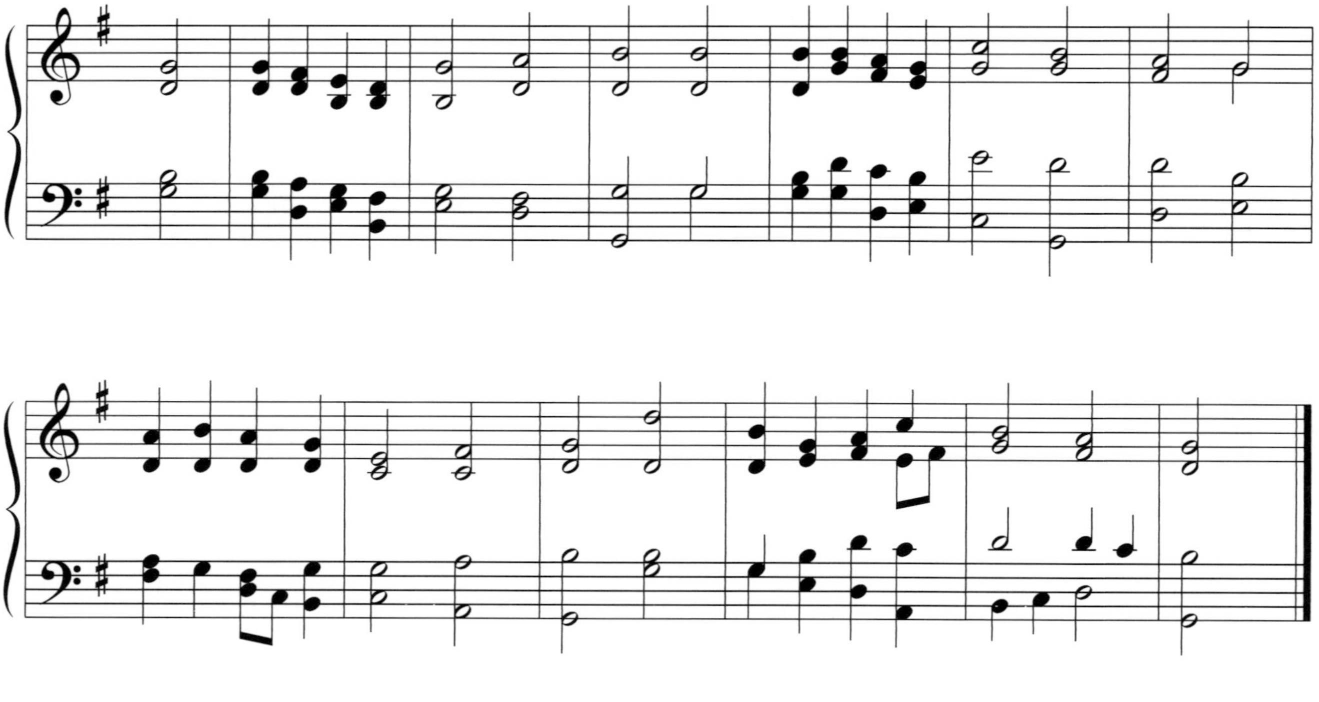

Nicaea

NICAEA
John B. Dykes, 1861

Passion Chorale

PASSION CHORALE
Harmonized by J.S. Bach, 1729

St. Theodulph

ST. THEODULPH
Melchior Teschner, 1615, arr. W. Monk, 1861

Azmon

AZMON
Lowell Mason, 1839

Canonbury

CANONBURY
Robert Schumannm, 1839

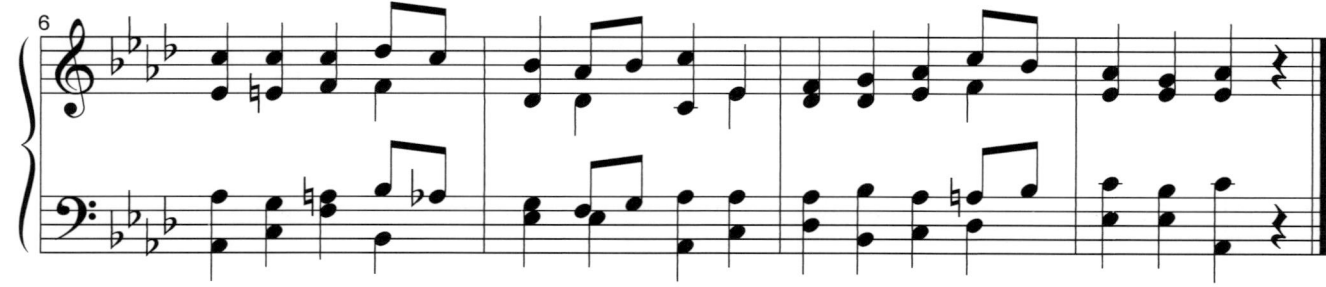

Crusaders' Hymn

CRUSADERS' HYMN
German, from *Schleischen Volksleider,* Leipsig, 1842

St. Anne

ST. ANNE
William Croft, 1708, arr. W. Monk, 1861

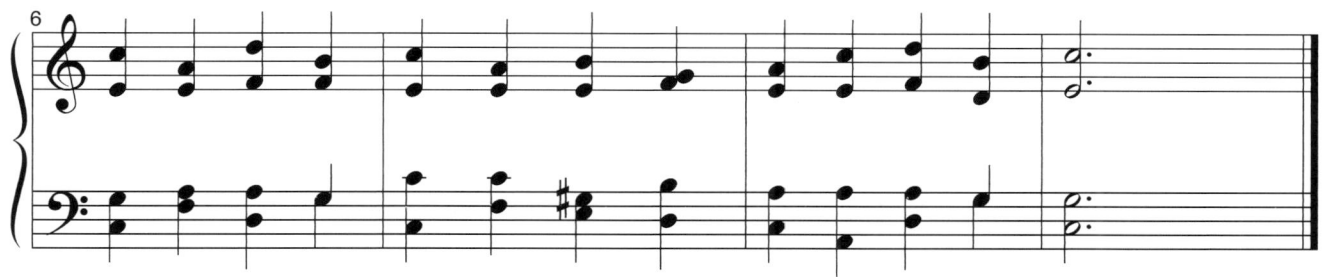

Hymn to Joy

HYMN TO JOY
arr. from L. van Beethoven by E. Hodges, 1864

Nun Danket Alle Gott

NUN DANKET
Johann Crüger, 1649, arr. F. Mendelssohn, 1840

Root Position Triads

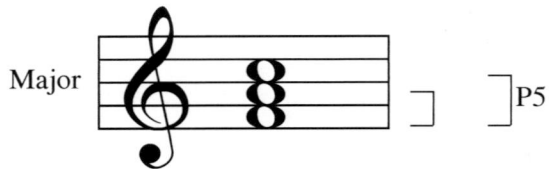
Major

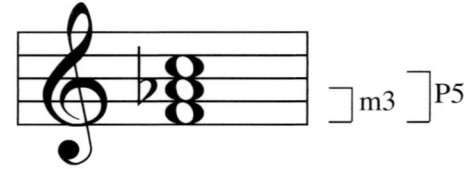

Use this fingering on all root position triads:

Right hand fingering: 1 3 5
Left hand fingering: 5 3 1

Here is the first set of triads (all the Major/minor triads on the white keys). If there is no accidental in front of a note then it should be considered a natural.

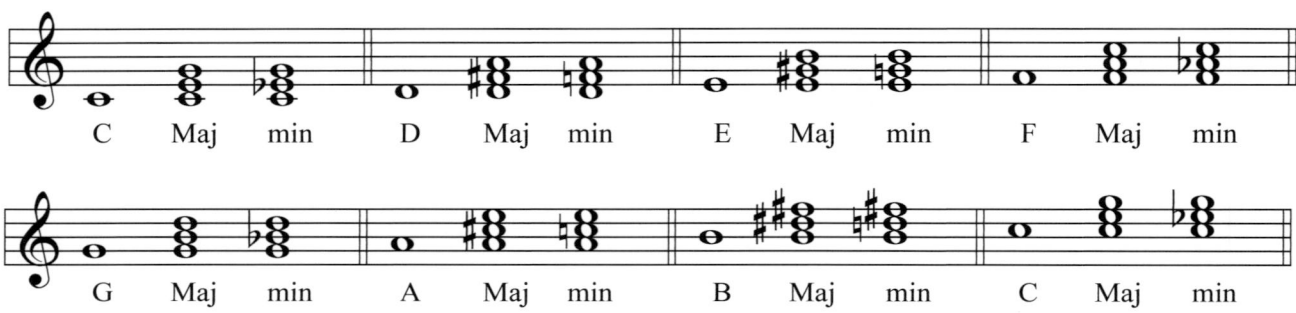

The next set of triads are all the Major/minor triads on the black notes. They are presented here in pairs, for example C#/D♭; D#/E♭, etc. For the purposes of actually playing the triad, it doesn't matter which version you use. For example, if A# Major triad seems complicated to you, then use its ENHARMONIC spelling, B♭ Major. If there is no accidental in front of a note then it should be considered a natural.

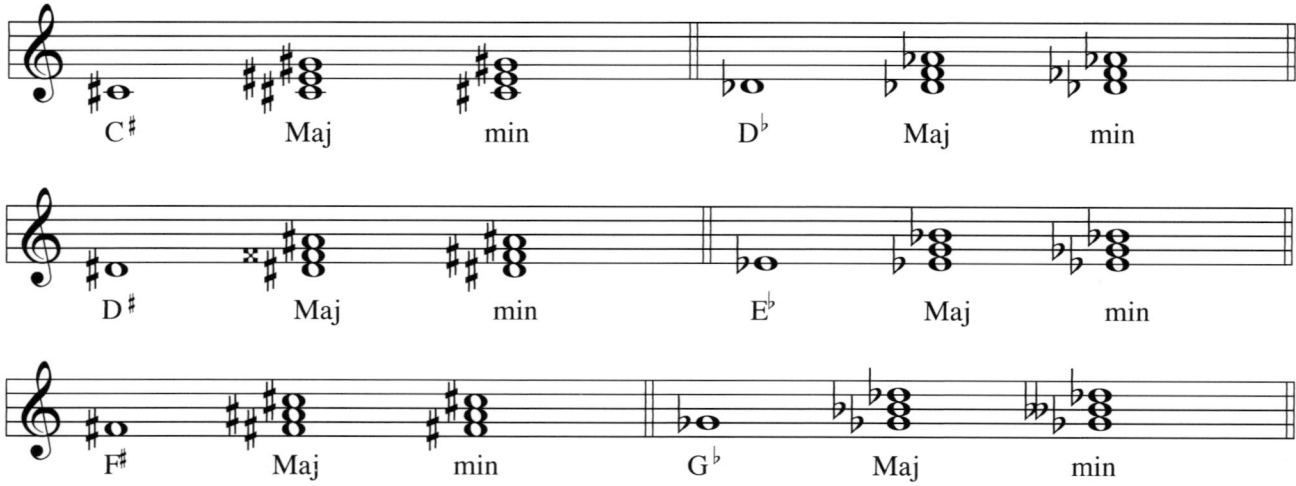

(Major/minor triads continued)

G♯
Maj
min
A♭
Maj
min
A♯
Maj
min
B♭
Maj
min

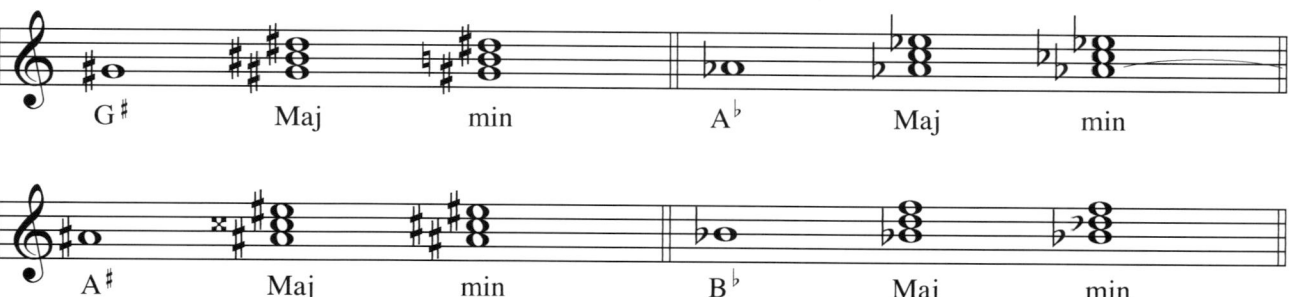

Here is a graphic representation of selected triads:

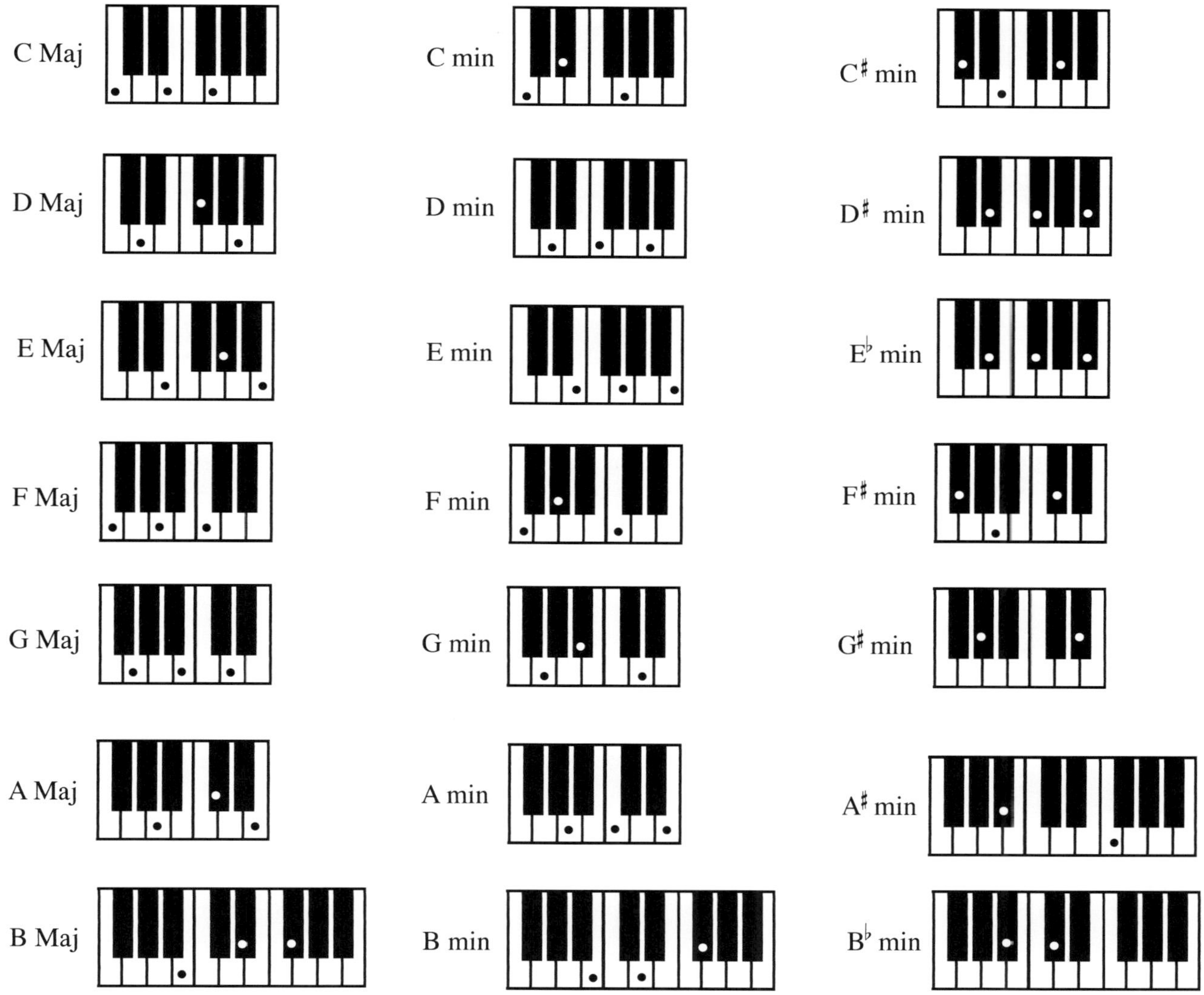

C Maj
C min
C♯ min
D Maj
D min
D♯ min
E Maj
E min
E♭ min
F Maj
F min
F♯ min
G Maj
G min
G♯ min
A Maj
A min
A♯ min
B Maj
B min
B♭ min

Root Position Triads, cont'd

Augmented triads are constructed from an Augmented 5th (A5) and a Major 3rd (M3); diminished triads are constructed from a diminished 5th (d5) and a minor 3rd (m3):

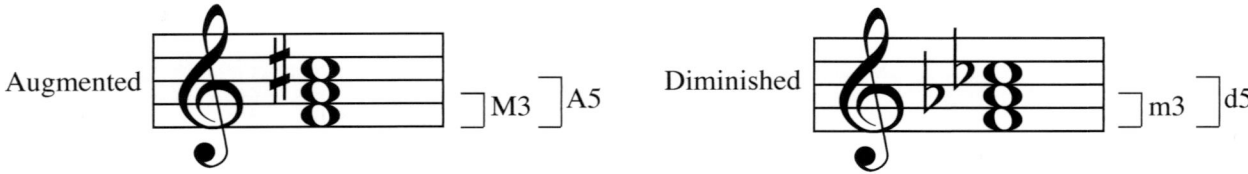

Use this fingering on all root position triads:

The third set of triads are all the Augmented/diminished triads on the white keys. If there is no accidental in front of a note then it should be considered a natural.

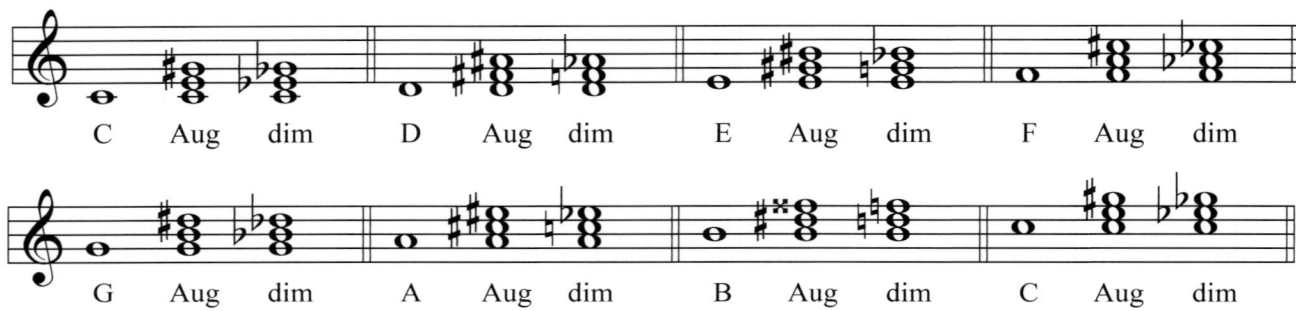

The final set of triads are all the Augmented/diminished triads on the black notes. They are presented here in pairs, for example: C#/D♭; D#/E♭, etc. For the purposes of actually playing the triad, it doesn't matter which version you use. For example, if A# Augmented triad seems complicated to you, then use its ENHARMONIC spelling, B♭ Augmented. If there is no accidental in front of a note then it should be considered a natural.

(Augmented/diminished triads continued)

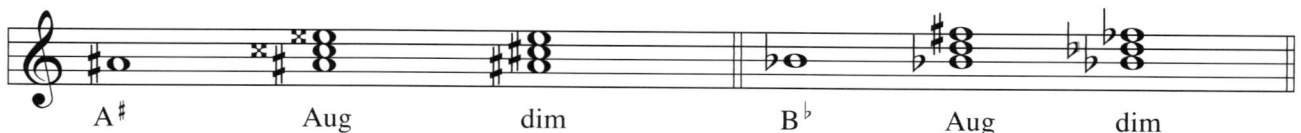

A♯   Aug   dim   B♭   Aug   dim

Here is a graphic representation of selected Augmented and diminished triads:

C Aug	C dim	C♯ Aug
D Aug	D dim	D♯ dim
E Aug	E dim	E♭ Aug
F Aug	F dim	F♯ dim
G Aug	G dim	G♯ dim
A Aug	A dim	A♯ Aug
B Aug	B dim	B♭ dim

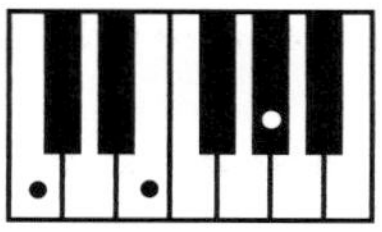

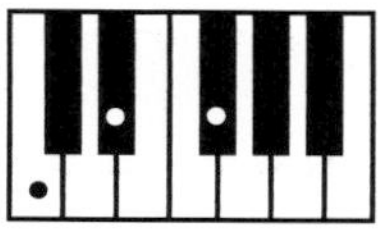

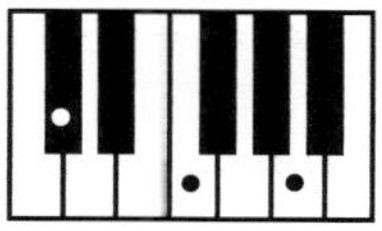

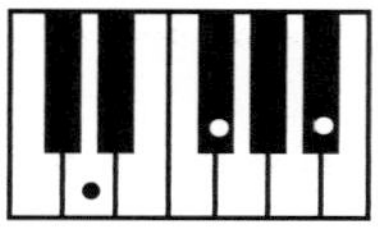

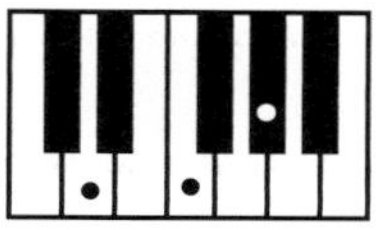

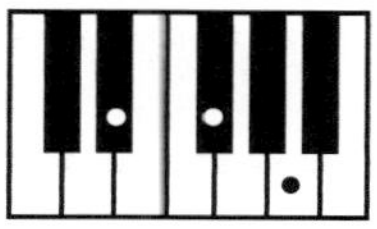

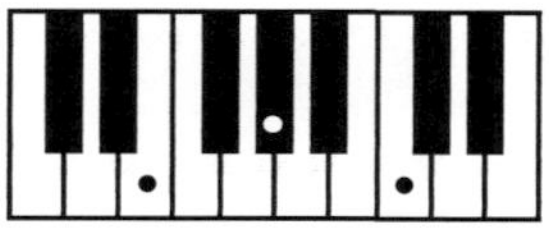

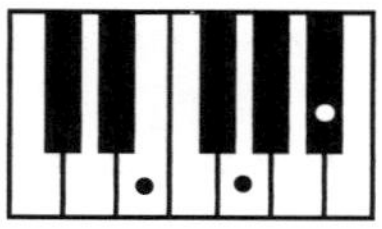

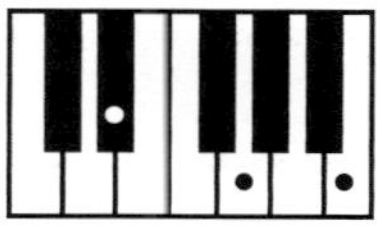

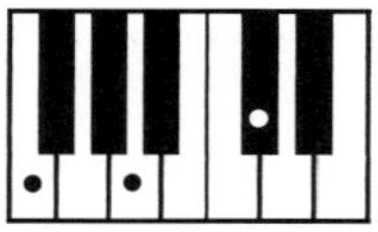

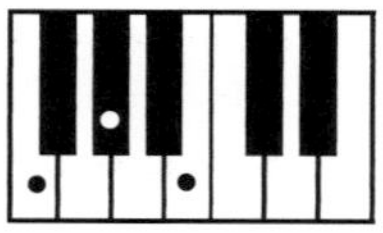

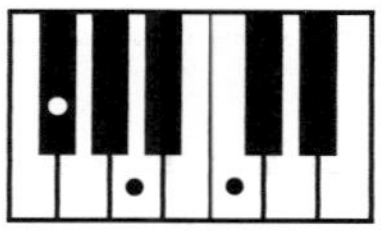

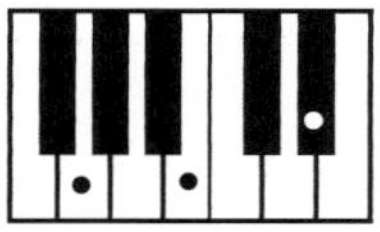

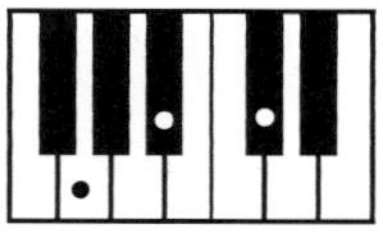

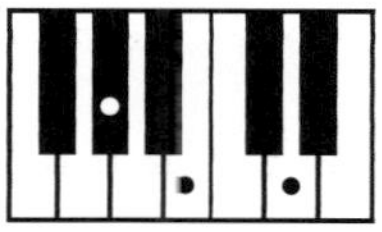

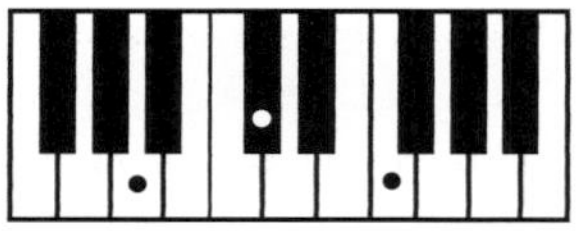

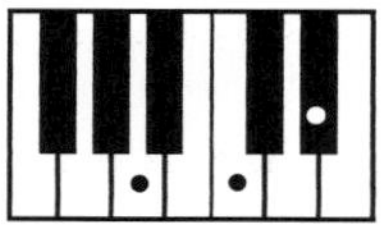

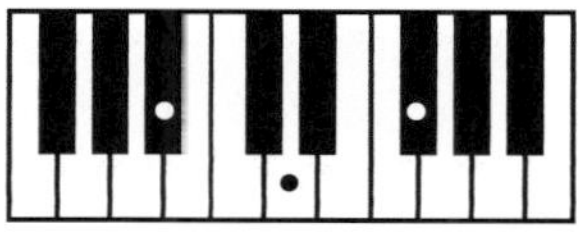

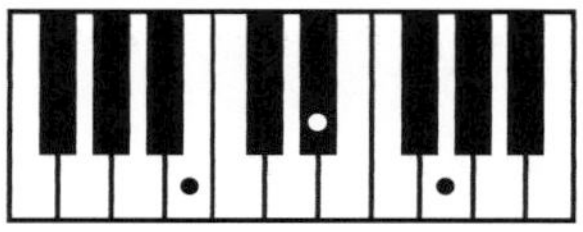

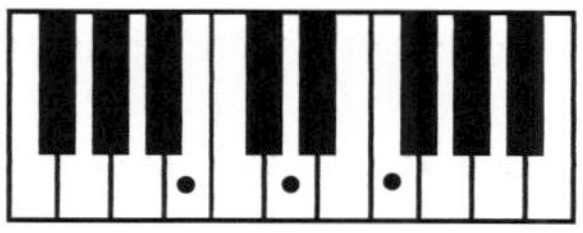

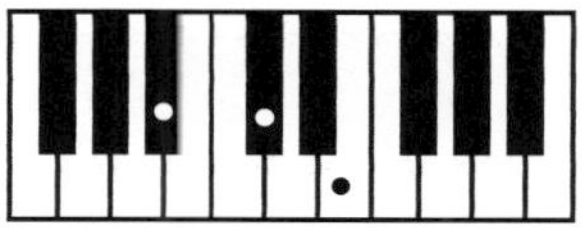

51

Procedures for Harmonizing Melodies

1. Memorize the appropriate cadence chord progression and be able to play it in the key of the melody.

2. Study carefully the material in Appendix 2 (Melodic Phrases), Appendix 3 (Melodic Cadences), and Appendix 4 (Non-Chord Tones).

3. Look through the melody and discover specific phrases and cadence points. Usually these can be found by doing one or more of the following:

   - look for the longest notes in the melody (see melody #35)
   - count 4 measures (see melody # 43)
   - look for repeated or similar phrases (see melody #11)
   - look for clearly defined TENSION/RELAXATION (see melody #1)
   - sing or play the melody and LISTEN for the tension/relaxation and points of rest (cadences).

4. Harmonize the cadence points at the ends of the phrases FIRST by WRITING IN THE CHORDS <u>for the cadence points.</u> You should do this before you harmonize the rest of the melody . Here are some general guidelines:

   Melodies with 2 phrases:

   - 1st phrase will usually end on a half cadence (usually on V, but sometimes on IV and sometimes on an IMPERFECT AUTHENTIC CADENCE, which Douglass Green calls a type of half cadence (see Appendix 2).
   - 2nd phrase will always be a conclusive cadence (cadence on I).

   Melodies with 4 phrases. There are many possible combinations but here is one possibility based on melody #20 (Minuet in G by Bach):

   - 1st phrase ends with an IMPERFECT AUTHENTIC CADENCE on the I chord.
   - 2nd phrase ends with a HALF CADENCE ON the V chord.
   - 3rd phrase (which is melodically similar to the 1st phrase) ends with an IMPERFECT AUTHENTIC CADENCE on the I chord.
   - 4th phrase (which is melodically similar to the 2nd phrase) ends with a CONCLUSIVE CADENCE which is a PERFECT AUTHENTIC CADENCE on the I chord.

   Melodies with 3 or 5 phrases: You will discover that the majority of successful melodies (see Appendix 2) have 2 or 4 phrases, each with a combination of 4 or 8 measures. However, many successful melodies have phrases with 6 measures (see AMERICA, p. 42) and there are melodies which have ODD numbers of phrases, for example, 3 phrases (see melody #1, "Twinkle, twinkle little star"); 5 phrases (see melody #42, "Aupres de ma blonde"). Nevertheless, you can find the specific cadence points by following the suggestions in #3 above.

5. Use a consistent harmonic rhythm. HARMONIC RHYTHM is a rhythmically strict progression of chords, for example one or two chords per measure. The harmonic rhythm may be anything that sounds good. However, the best harmonic rhythm depends upon such factors as tempo, style, etc. A typical harmonic rhythm would be either one or two chords per measure.   Also, tempo affects decisions regarding the harmonic rhythm.

Generally, if the tempo is fast then use a slower harmonic rhythm. If the tempo is slow then use a faster harmonic rhythm. If you decide on a harmonic rhythm of two chords per measure, it is sometimes a good idea to use the same chord twice. YOU DON'T ALWAYS HAVE TO CHANGE CHORDS. Keep it simple.

6. Write in the chords for the rest of the melody. Remember, KEEP IT SIMPLE. Make your chord progression "culminate" at the cadence points you already wrote in. They should "make sense" musically.

7. Using SECONDARY DOMINANTS. The most common secondary dominant is V^7/V and probably the best place to use V^7/V is right before the V chord at a half cadence. For example:

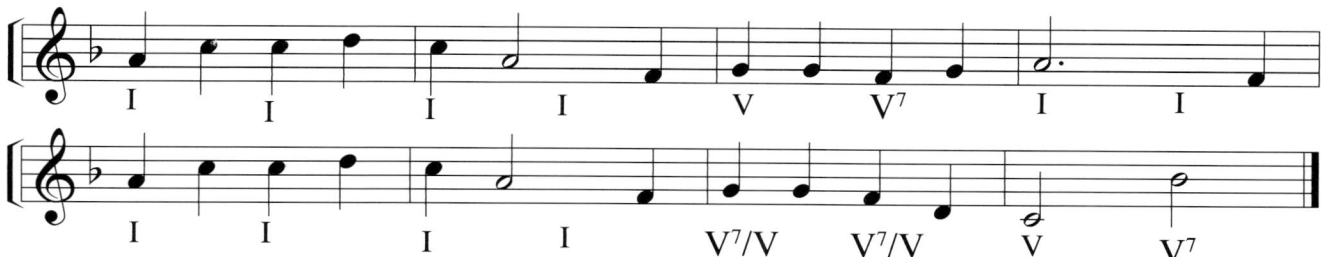

In this melody segment (part of melody # 34, "Go tell it on the mountain"), the 2nd phrase is definitely a half cadence on V and the use of the V^7/V chord in the next to last measure creates a particularly strong cadence.

Some other points to notice in this harmonization:

- The harmonic rhythm is a half note (2 chords per measure).

- There is much repetition of the I chord at the beginning of both the 1st and 2nd phrase and this is OK! You don't have to change chords on every beat. Keep it simple.

- The use of a V^7 on beat 3 of the 3rd measure might seem wrong because the F is not part of the V^7 chord. However, this is an example of an ACCENTED LOWER NEIGHBOR TONE. In other words, it's a NON-CHORD TONE (see Appendix 4). If you use a I chord on the 3rd beat it sounds "weak" because the harmonic movement: V^7 - I works best when it is in a "weak/strong" juxtaposition. For example, the word "to-DAY" has the 2nd syllable accented (weak/STRONG). If the 1st syllable was accented instead, it would sound "weird" : TO-day (STRONG/weak). The V^7 - I progression has this kind of relationship: weak to STRONG and that's why it is better to have the I chord of a V^7 - I progression happen on a STRONG beat, particularly beat ONE.

8. More on secondary dominants:

- V^7/V goes to V (that's why it's called "five-seven of FIVE". The Beatles use of V^7/V not withstanding, the V^7/V does not go to I and will be considered wrong in these harmonizations.

- Generally any secondary dominant resolves to it's "ultimate chord." For example V^7/ii resolves to ii; V^7/iii resolves to iii, etc. However, any secondary dominant can also resolve to a SUBSTITUTION chord instead. For example, V^7/ii can (and often does) resolve to V^7/V. Consequently, this sets up a nice chord progression where the roots of the various chords resolve in a "chain" of (perfect) 4ths. See the last phrase of melody #55 where there is this progression of chords: V^7/vi -- V^7/ii -- V^7/V -- I.

Block-Chord Cadences

"Block-chord" means all chords are **voiced** with 3 notes in each hand and each chord is identified by its Roman Numeral, not by its inversion. The following are "block-chord" style cadences. Here, "cadence" means a succession of chords (such as I-IV-I-V7-I) and does not refer to what happes at the end of a phrase as described in Appendix 3 (page 110).

*The Roman numerals in this section refer to the basic chords and not to specific inversions.

Cadences, cont'd: V⁷/V

*The Roman numerals in this section refer to the basic chords and not to specific inversions.

Cadences, cont'd: V⁷/ii in Major; V7/III in Minor

*The Roman numerals in this section refer to the basic chords and not to specific inversions.

Cadences, cont'd: V^7/IV (iv)

*The Roman numerals in this section refer to the basic chords and not to specific inversions.

Accompaniment Patterns

One way to harmonize a melody is to simply use the BLOCK-CHORDS from the cadences (pp. 56 - 59). However, a more interesting accompaniment can be accomplished by superimposing patterns on the block-chords as demonstrated below:

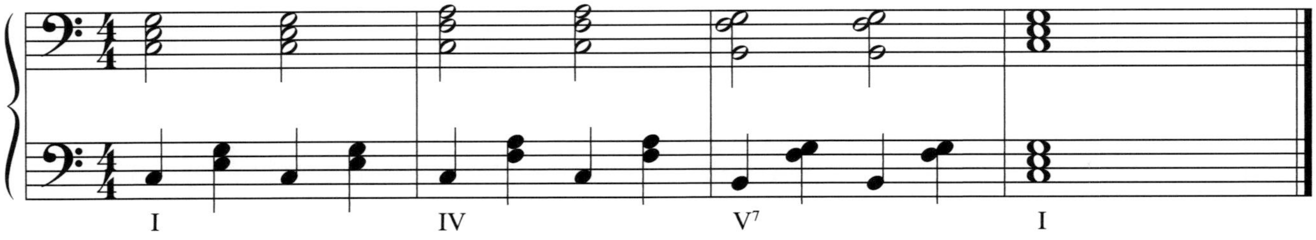

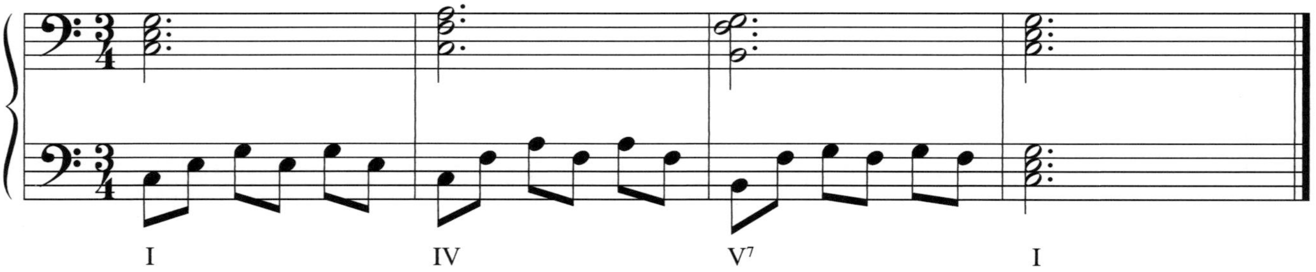

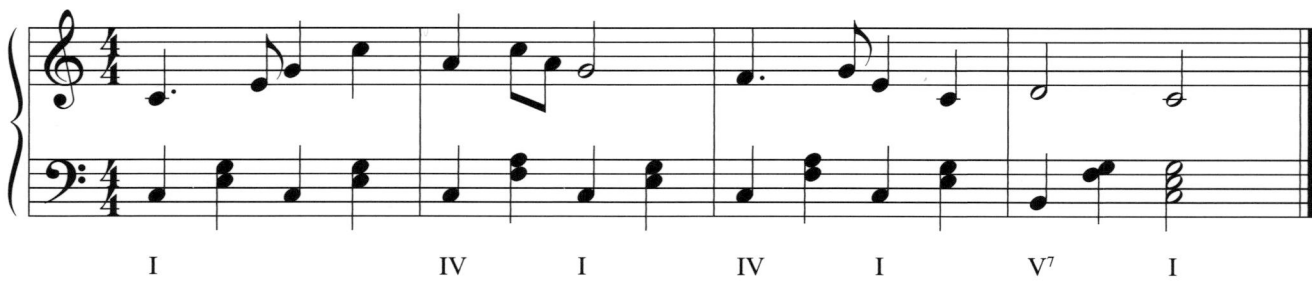

Here's an actual melody written out using Accompaniment Pattern #1. See melody #22 in the next section.

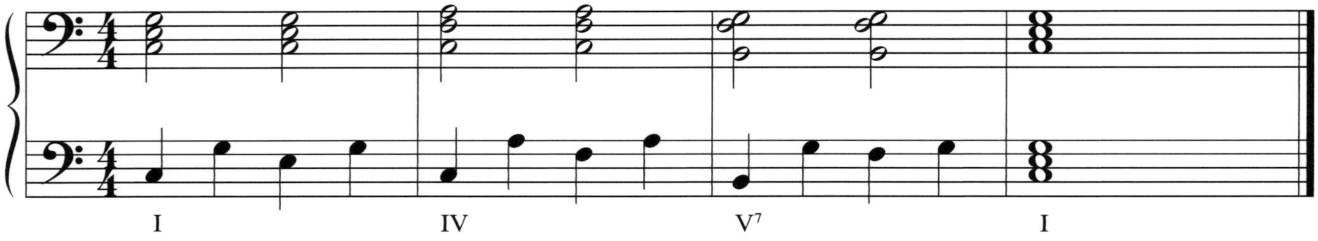

Known colloquially as the "um-pah" or "boom-chick" pattern, this accompaniment has been used successfully by many composers, particularly in early twentieth century popular styles (ragtime, stride, etc.). Here's an excerpt from the melody of a Scott Joplin Rag using a simple "um-pah" pattern accompaniment:

The above example is not the actual accompaniment by Joplin but shows how a basic cadence voicing can be combined with an accompaniment pattern to produce a very "respectable" arrangement. Below IS an excerpt from an actual Joplin Rag (**Peacherine Rag**, p. 27). Compare it to the accompaniment above and notice how the basic "um-pah" pattern has been expanded to "full" chords with an alternating bass note.

The simple accompaniment:

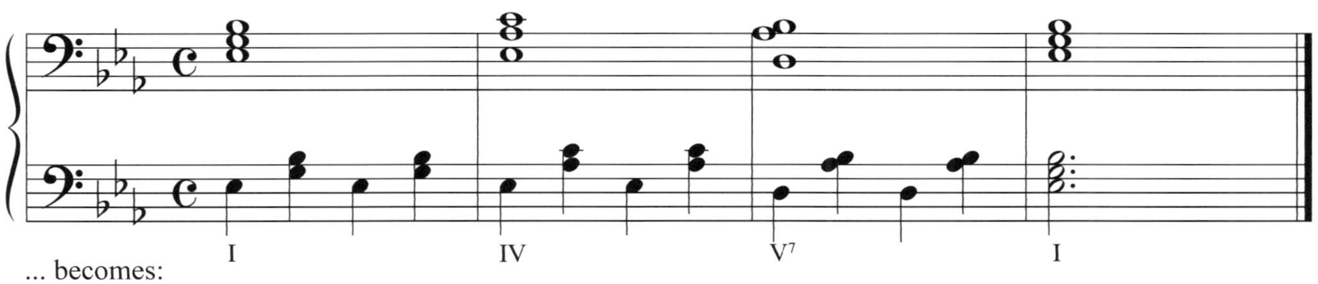

... becomes:

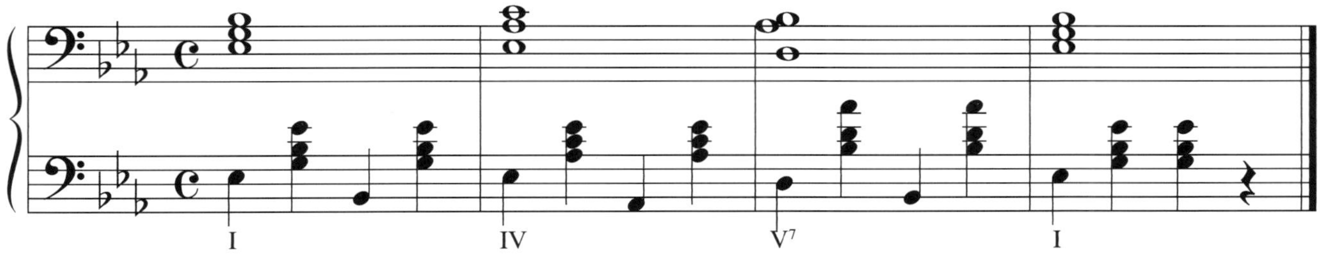

Melodies for Harmonization

66

68

FORREST GREEN
English Folk Song

38

HOM ON THE RANGE
American Folk Song

39

WE SHALL OVERCOME
Negro Spiritual

40

German Folk Song

41

Improvisation

The goal for improvisation skills in Secondary Piano is to improvise simple melodies over a given chord progression. In Level Four the improvisation examples will consist of:

1. Primary chords and some secondary dominants: V7/V in major and minor keys, V7/ii in major keys, V7/IV in major keys, V7/iv in minor keys -- all required keys are through two accidentals.
2. Improvised melodies should consist mainly of chord tones, passing tones, and neighbor tones. Some accented non-chord tones may be used, especially accented passing tones and appoggiaturas. See Appendix IV for a complete explanation of non-chord tones.
3. The range of the improvisation should be about an octave.
4. Improvised melodies should generally make use of a RHYTHMIC MOTIVE (see below).
5. Non-motivic melodic construction concepts will also be encouraged.
6. Use a consistent HARMONIC RHYTHM (for example, 1 or 2 chords per measure).

Improvisation involves spontaneously making up a melody over a given chord progression. The chord voicings required in Level Four piano will be the same as those found in the block-chord cadences earlier in this book, especially Cadence #4. All the improvisation examples in Level Four piano will involve improvising melodies consisting of a combination of chord tones and non-chord tones. Here is a written-out example demonstrating basic requirements for this level:

Consider the following example:

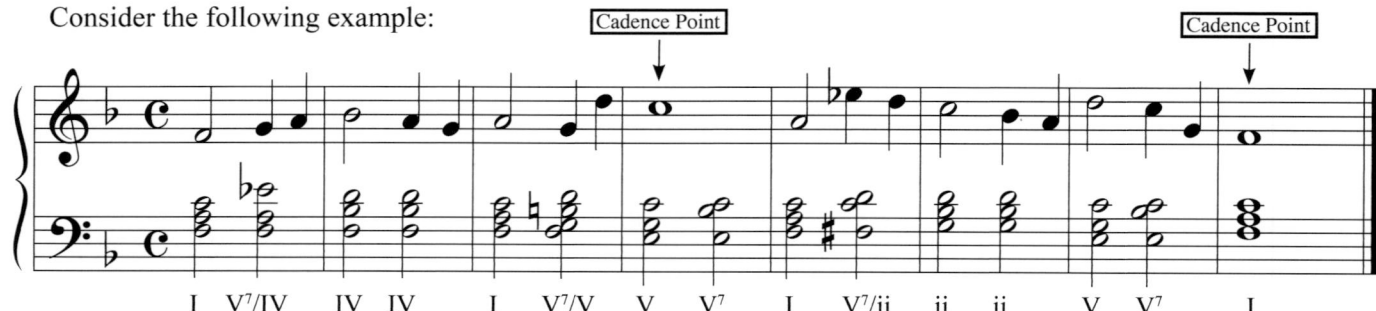

In the above example the melody notes consist of chord tones, accented passing tones, and appoggiaturas. Note the use of the secondary dominants V7/IV in measure 1, V7/V in measure 3, and V7/ii in measure 5. Also notice how the rhythm for the melody is the same in each measure except for the whole notes in measures 4 and 8. This repetitive rhythm is called a "rhythm motive" and the whole notes in measures 4 and 8 are at CADENCE POINTS (see Appendix 2 and 3 at the end of this book for a detailed explanation of melodic phrases and cadences). Accented non-chord tones are used in almost every measure. It is OK to use dissonant notes on accented beats as long as they are resolved correctly. If you do not understand non-chord tones or cannot recognize them, ask your instructor for an explanation. Also, see **Appendix IV** for an explanation.

The short example above is a complete melody and consists of TWO PHRASES. The PHRASES are set apart by the whole notes in measures 4 and 8 and these POINTS OF REST within the melody are called CADENCES. It is often easy to find the CADENCE POINTS in any melody -- just look for the longest note values, particularly if they occur in groups of 4 or 8 measures. FOUR-MEASURE PHRASES are very common in all styles of Western music. You can make your improvised melodies sound like "real" melodies if you structure them like REAL MELODIES:

1. Use a simple rhythmic motive.
2. Use LONG NOTES (whole notes, dotted whole notes, etc.) at the cadence points.
3. Superimpose your rhythmic motive on TWO consecutive chords.
4. Always end with the tonic note (1st degree of the scale). The majority of successful melodies in

western music end on the tonic note. "Successful melodies" are those melodies which have been IN USE for a long period of time, for example, 50 years, 100 years, etc. Look through the melodies in the Harmonized Melodies section of this book and you will discover that they ALL end on the tonic note.

The goal for Level Four Piano is to be able to improvise using chord tones, passing tones, and neighbor tones over a given chord progression. Try improvising a melody over the following chords. The first measure has been done for you and you should use the rhythmic MOTIVE written in the first measure, in each subsequent measure throughout the example except at the cadence points where you see the whole notes.

Improvise a melody for the following example using the rhythmic motive in first measure. Experiment with using some accented non-chord tones. Repeat in the keys of C and F. Use long notes (whole notes) at the cadence points.

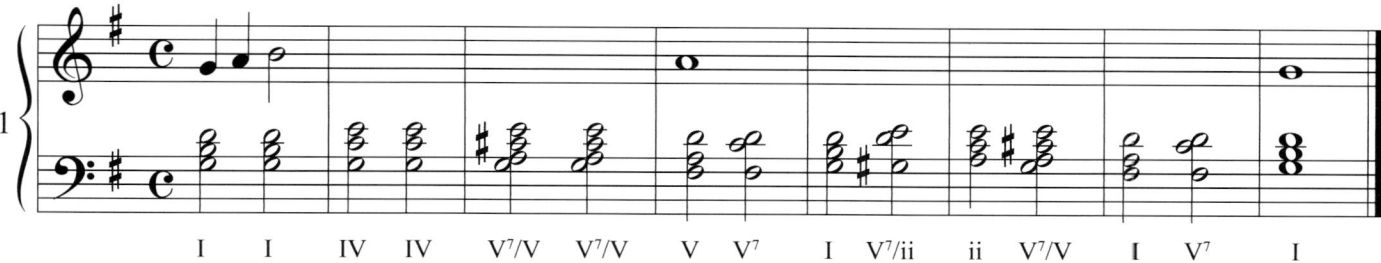

Do:

1. Use chord tones, passing tones, neighbor tones, and accented non chord tones. If you need to, consult the example on the previous page.
2. Generally, keep the overall range of your improvisation within about an octave. You may want to start out with a limited range of a 4th or 5th and then gradually increase the range to an octave.
3. If you have trouble with the coordination aspect, try "patting" the rhythm of the right hand while you play the chords in the left hand. It's always a good idea to practice counting out-loud while you play.
4. Try starting your improvisation on a scale degree other than the 1st scale degree (for example the 3rd of the 5th).

Don't:

1. Don't write out your improvisation. Make it up (improvise it) every time.

When you feel comfortable playing the example above in the written key of G major, try playing it in the major keys of C, F, D, and B-flat,

Improvise a melody for the following example using the rhythmic motive in first measure. Repeat in the major keys of C, G, D, and B-flat. Use long notes (whole notes) at the cadence points.

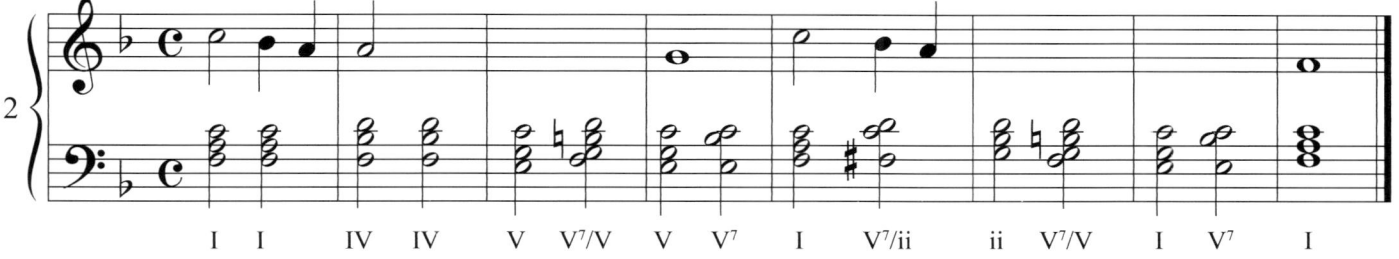

Improvisation, Part II: More on Rhythmic Motives

As described earlier, a MOTIVE is a short melodic and/or rhythmic idea used as a constructional element. Many successful melodies use non-motivic melodic construction. However, the efforts of novice improvisers to play non-motivic improvisations often sound "rambling" -- that is, the improvised melody sounds random, not having any real direction, strong cadence points, sense of tension/relaxation, or climax. An improvised melody has the potential of having a greater sense of unity and direction (climax and cadence) if it is constructed motivically, especially for someone just learning to improvise.

To begin to develop a concept of rhythmic motive, write out four (4) one-measure rhythmic motives for each of the meters below. Individual melody notes are inconsequential at this point. The actual melody notes will later be determined by the given chords. For now, use any pitches you want or just use one pitch. To be VIABLE your rhythmic motive must have at least TWO different rhythmic values, for example a half note and 2 quarter notes. Consequently, 4 quarter notes, 2 half notes, 8 eighth notes, etc. would not be viable rhythmic motives. Your rhythmic motives will be ONE measure long and will be the equivalent of 2 chords in length. For example, in 4/4/ time each chord would get 2 beats and there would be 2 chords in each measure; in 6/4 time each chord would get 3 beats and there would be 2 chords in each measure.

After you have completed the composition of your rhythmic motives, improvise complete melodies over the example chord progressions below by making use of one of your motives. Use ONE motive for the entire improvisation. Use a LONG note (whole note or dotted whole note) at the cadence points. Before you begin, analyze the chords and write them in the music below the chords. <u>DO NOT</u> WRITE OUT YOUR IMPROVISATION IN THE MUSIC, but you may sketch out your chosen rhythmic motive in the provided treble clef.

Improvisation: Improvised Melodies Over Chord Symbols (general review)

When you improvise melodies over chord progressions the voicings of the chords you play in the left hand should be the same as the cadence chords you have already learned. However, if your instructor agrees you may use any voicings you wish as long as you keep the rhythm correct and the tempo steady.

Practice the examples in the required keys for your cadences (through 2 accidentals). Each example is two phrases (2 lines) long. The next-to-last chord in each phrase is the CADENCE POINT. Please follow these rules:

1. Play the cadence for the key in which you plan to improvise.
2. Play through the chord progression with just the left hand using the cadence voicings.
3. Use one of the rhythmic motives you wrote out on the previous page.
4. Play the chord progression with your left hand while you PAT the rhythmic motive with your right.
5. Play LONG notes (one note that lasts for 2 chords) at all the CADENCE POINTS.
6. Keep the range of your improvisation within an octave, although you might start off with a range of a 4th or 5th and then gradually increase it to an octave
7. Create your improvisation using chord tones, passing tones, neighbor tones and appogiaturas.
8. Generally, it is better to use more steps than skips.
9. Always end the improvisation on the tonic note.

For all these chord progressions:

1. Prepare each one TWICE: once with 2 beats for each chord and once with 3 beats for each chord.

2. Use one of the rhythmic motives you composed on the previous page.

3. The CADENCE POINT for each phrase is the next-to-last chord in each line. So, play a LONG note on that chord and don't continue your rhythmic motive. See the example at the beginning of this section as a model.

4. It's always a good idea to practice playing the chords with the left hand while you PAT your rhythmic motive with the right hand.

Improvisation, Part III: Non-Motivic Melodic Construction.

Creating a successful non-motivic improvisation is more challenging than using motivic construction. Here are a few basic principles which will help in improvising non-motivic melodies.

Consider the following examples:

COME SUNDAY
Duke Ellington, 1946

Copyright 1946, 1966 by Tempo Music Inc., New York, New York. Used by Permission.

SONG 13
Orlando Gibbons, 1623

The first melody, COME SUNDAY (composed in 1946 by Duke Ellington), is constructed non-motivically. The second melody, SONG 13 (composed in 1623 by Orlando Gibbons), makes use of motivic construction. Both melodies consist of four phrases and both melodies use longer note values at the cadence points. COME SUNDAY has more rhythmic diversity and this is the key to constructing interesting and effective melodies which do not make use of motivic construction. THE MOST INTERESTING NON-MOTIVIC MELODIES ARE THOSE WHICH HAVE RHYTHMIC DIVERSITY, that is, different rhythmic combinations in each measure.

The absolute opposite of this are melodies which use only a single rhythmic value throughout, as in the following melody.

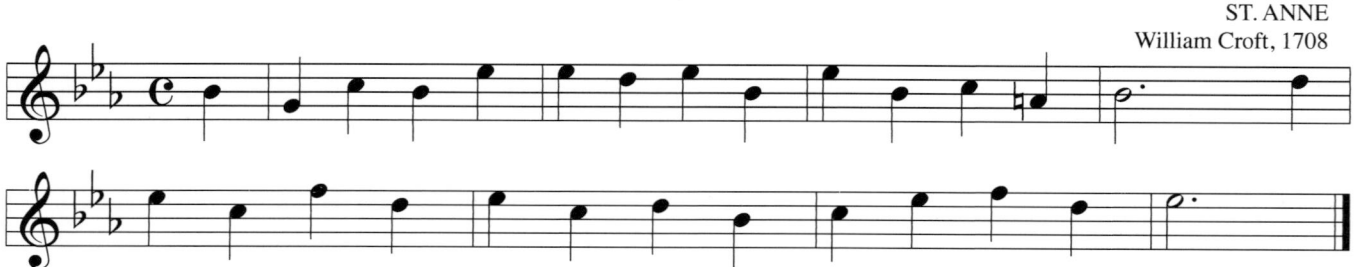

ST. ANNE
William Croft, 1708

ST. ANNE has proved to be one of the most successful melodies ever written despite its static rhythm. However, what it lacks in rhythmic diversity it makes up in strong cadence points, interesting intervals and climax. The melodic interval of a 4th is used 8 times throughout the tune and this tends to reinforce a strong sense of cadence. In addition, the overall angular intervallic motion (a descending interval followed by an ascending interval) gives a unique feel to the tune which makes it memorable.

Here are some general guidelines for creating tunes which are not constructed motivically:

1. Strive for rhythmic diversity (different rhythms in each measure)
2. Have clearly defined cadence points. The melody note at the actual cadence point should be the longest note value of the phrase.
3. The melody should have a sense of climax. Often this is accomplished with the highest note of the melody occurring only once at the point of climax.

Points 2 and 3 above also apply to motivic melodies but are particularly true for non-motivic melodies. Otherwise, there is a strong tendency for non-motivic melodies to degenerate into rambling bits of nonsense.

Improvise non-motivic melodies over the given chord progressions below. Before you begin, analyze the chords and write them in the music below the chords. <u>DO NOT</u> WRITE OUT YOUR IMPROVISATION IN THE MUSIC, but you may sketch out rhythmic ideas in the provided treble clef.

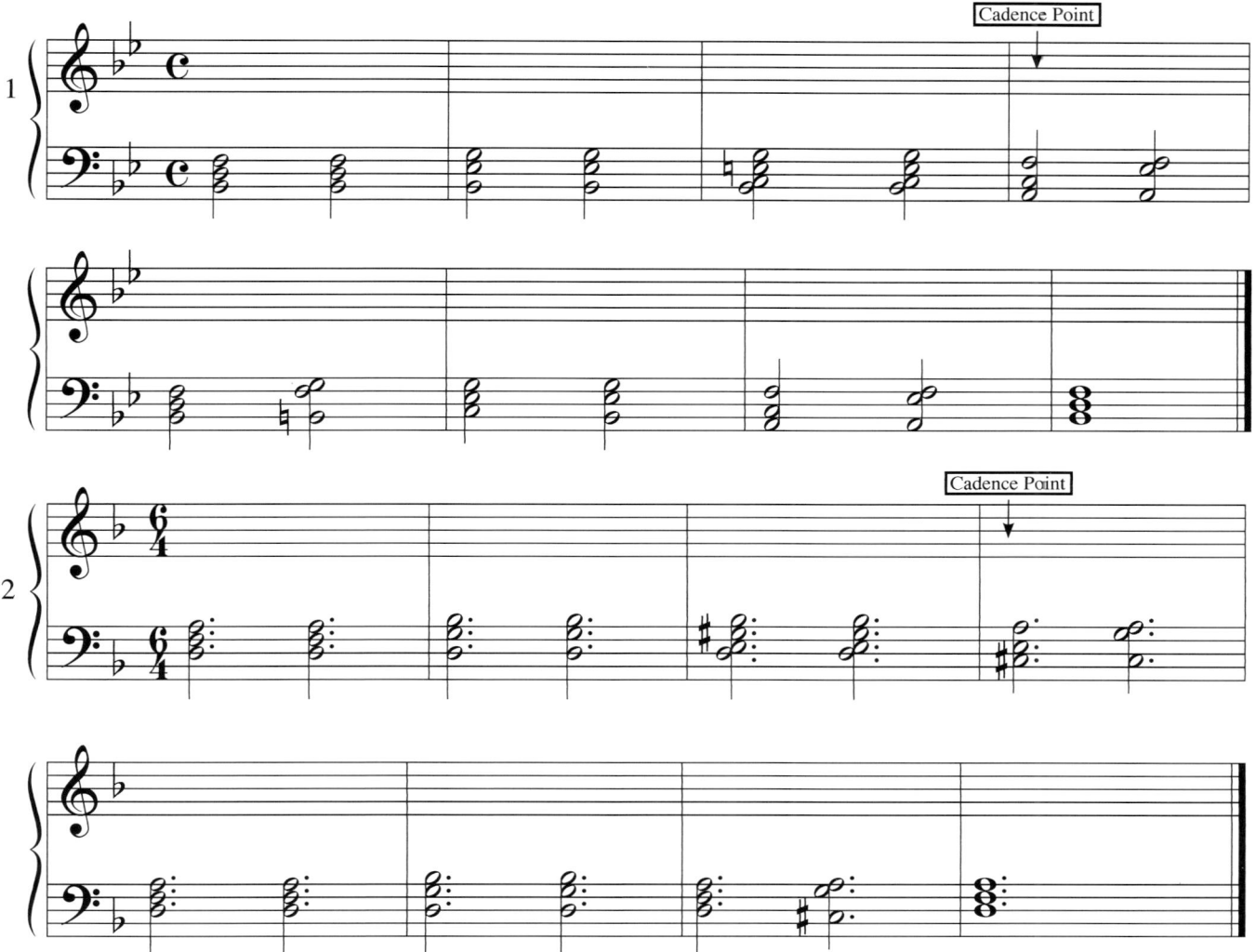

Improvisation, Review from Level III: Primary Chords and Secondary Dominants: V^7/V, V^7/ii

Before you practice the improvisation requirements for Level IV on the next page you may have to review the chord progressions from Level III (primary chords and two secondary dominants -- V^7/V, V^7/ii

Play each example in the following keys:

    Major: C D F G B♭
    Minor: am bm dm em gm

Each example is two phrases (2 lines) long. You should prepare each improvisation twice: once giving each chord 2 beats, and once giving each chord 3 beats.

Please follow these procedures:

1. Play the cadence for the key in which you plan to improvise.
2. Play through the chord progression with just the left hand using the cadence voicings.
3. Use one of the rhythmic motives you wrote out earlier in this section.
4. Play the chord progression with your left hand while you PAT the rhythmic motive with your right.
5. Play LONG notes (one note that lasts for 2 chords) at all the CADENCE POINTS.
6. Keep the range of your improvisation within a 5th or 6th (although you might start off with a range of a 3rd or 4th).
7. Create your improvisation using chord tones, passing tones, and neighbor tones..
8. Generally, it is better to use more steps than skips.
9, Always end the improvisation on the tonic note

							Cadence Point ↓	
1	I	I	IV	IV	I	V^7/V	V	V^7
	I	V^7/ii	ii	V^7/V	V	V^7	I	I
2	i	i	iv	iv	i	V^7/V	V	V^7
	i	i	iv	iv	i	V^7	i	i
3	I	IV	I	I	IV	V^7/V	V	V^7
	I	V^7/ii	ii	V	I	V^7	I	I
4	i	iv	i	i	iv	V^7/V	V	V^7
	i	V^7/V	V	V^7	i	V^7	i	i
5	I	V^7/ii	ii	V^7/V	V	V^7/V	V	V^7
	I	V^7/ii	ii	V^7/V	V	V^7	I	I

Improvisation, Requirement for Level IV: Secondary Dominants: V^7/V, V^7/ii, V^7/IV, V^7/iv

Improvise melodies over the following chord progressions using any combination of techniques you have learned so far. The voicings you should use for the chords are the same voicings you have learned for the cadences earlier in this book. However, if your instructor agrees you may use any voicing you wish as long as you keep the rhythm correct and the tempo steady. For example, give each chord the correct number of beats.

Play each example in the following keys:

    Major: C D F G B♭
    Minor: am bm dm em gm

Each example is two phrases (2 lines) long. You should prepare each improvisation twice: once giving each chord 2 beats, and once giving each chord 3 beats.

Please follow these procedures:

1. Play the cadence for the key in which you plan to improvise.
2. Play through the chord progression with just the left hand using the cadence voicings.
3. Use one of the rhythmic motives you wrote out earlier in this section.
4. Play the chord progression with your left hand while you PAT the rhythmic motive with your right.
5. Play LONG notes (one note that lasts for 2 chords) at all the CADENCE POINTS.
6. Keep the range of your improvisation within an octave, although you might start off with a range of a 4th or 5th and then gradually increase it to an octave.
7. Create your improvisation using chord tones, passing tones, neighbor tones, and appogiaturas.
8. Generally, it is better to use more steps than skips.
9, Always end the improvisation on the tonic note

Cadence Point ↓ (above column 7)

1.
| I | I | IV | IV | I | V^7/V | V | V^7 |
| I | V^7/IV | IV | IV | I | V^7 | I | I |

2.
| i | i | iv | iv | i | V^7/V | V | V^7 |
| i | V^7/iv | iv | iv | i | V^7 | i | i |

3.
| I | V^7/IV | IV | IV | V | V^7/V | V | V^7 |
| I | V^7/ii | ii | V^7/V | V | V^7 | I | I |

4.
| i | V^7/iv | iv | iv | V | V^7/V | V | V^7 |
| i | V^7/iv | iv | iv | i | V^7 | i | i |

5.
| I | V^7/ii | ii | V^7/V | V | V^7/V | V | V^7 |
| I | V^7/IV | IV | IV | V | V^7 | I | I |

Sight Reading and Transposition I: Piano Scores

88

DUET IN G MINOR
WDL

ODE TO JOY
Beethoven, arr. WDL

Music © 2001 by Smith Creek Music, Nashville, TN 37214. All rights reserved. www.smithcreekmusic.com

93

LITTLE WALTZ
WDL

35

AWAY IN A MANGER
arr. WDL

36

Music © 2001 by Smith Creek Music, Nashville, TN 37214. All rights reserved. www.smithcreekmusic.com

Sight Reading and Transposition II: Open Scores

from *Gloria*
Antonio Vivaldi

Anonymous
c. 1600

Music © 2001 by Smith Creek Music, Nashville, TN 37214. All rights reserved. www.smithcreekmusic.com

97

Ave Maria
Jacob Arcadelt

IN BABILONE
Traditional Dutch Melody

Music © 2001 by Smith Creek Music, Nashville, TN 37214. All rights reserved. www.smithcreekmusic.com

G. F. Handel

from *Cosi fan Tutti*
W.A. Mozart

Canzon
Wm. Brade

7

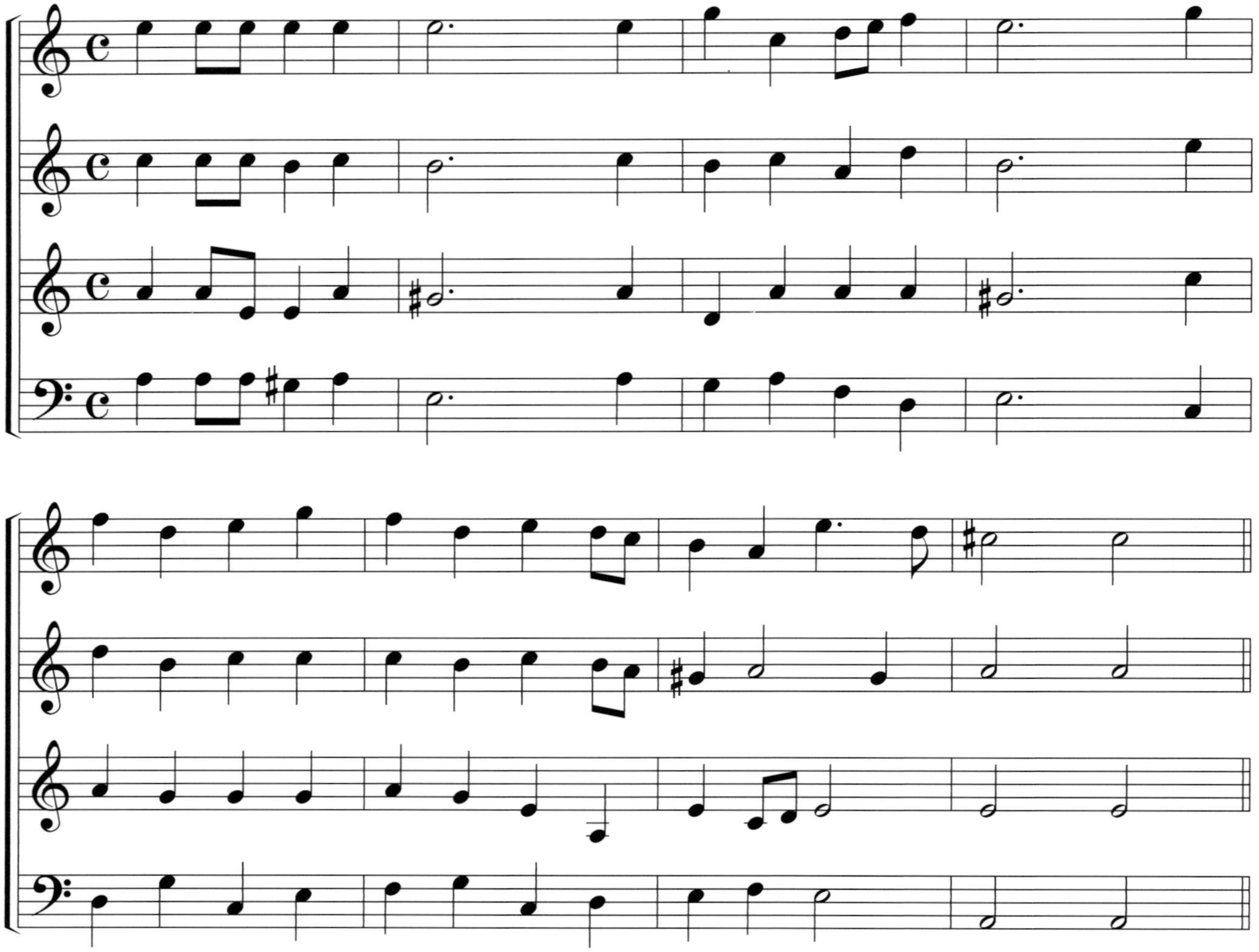

from *Christmas Oratorio*
Saint-Saëns

8

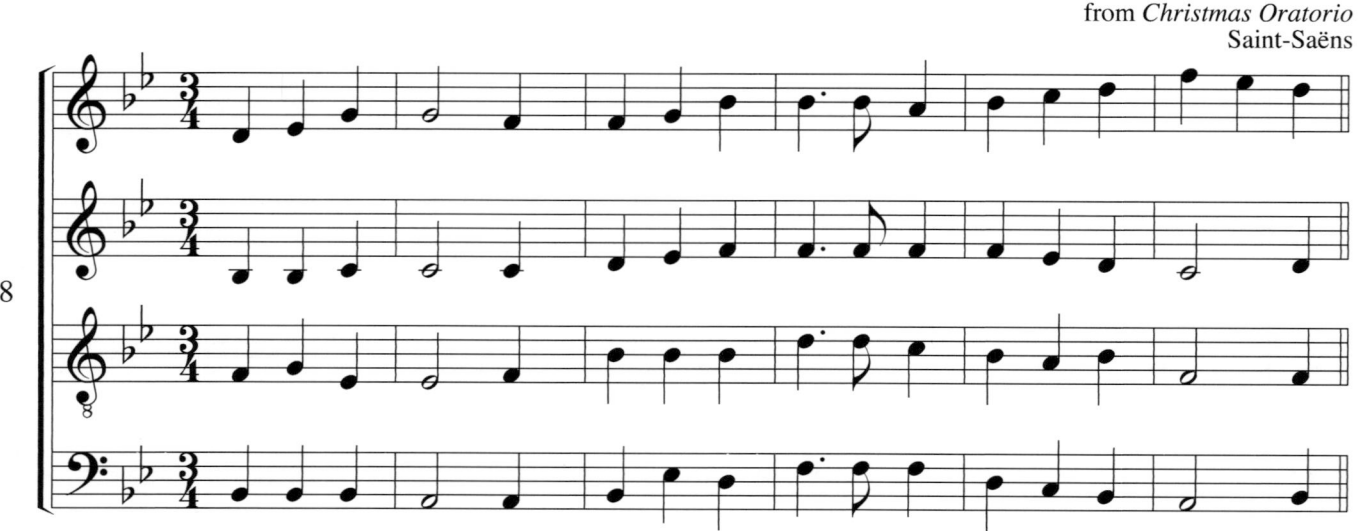

Trio
Bernardo Pisano

Lo, How a Rose e'er Blooming
Michael Praetorius

Open Score #11

from *l'Oiseau de Feu*, 1910
Igor Stravinsky

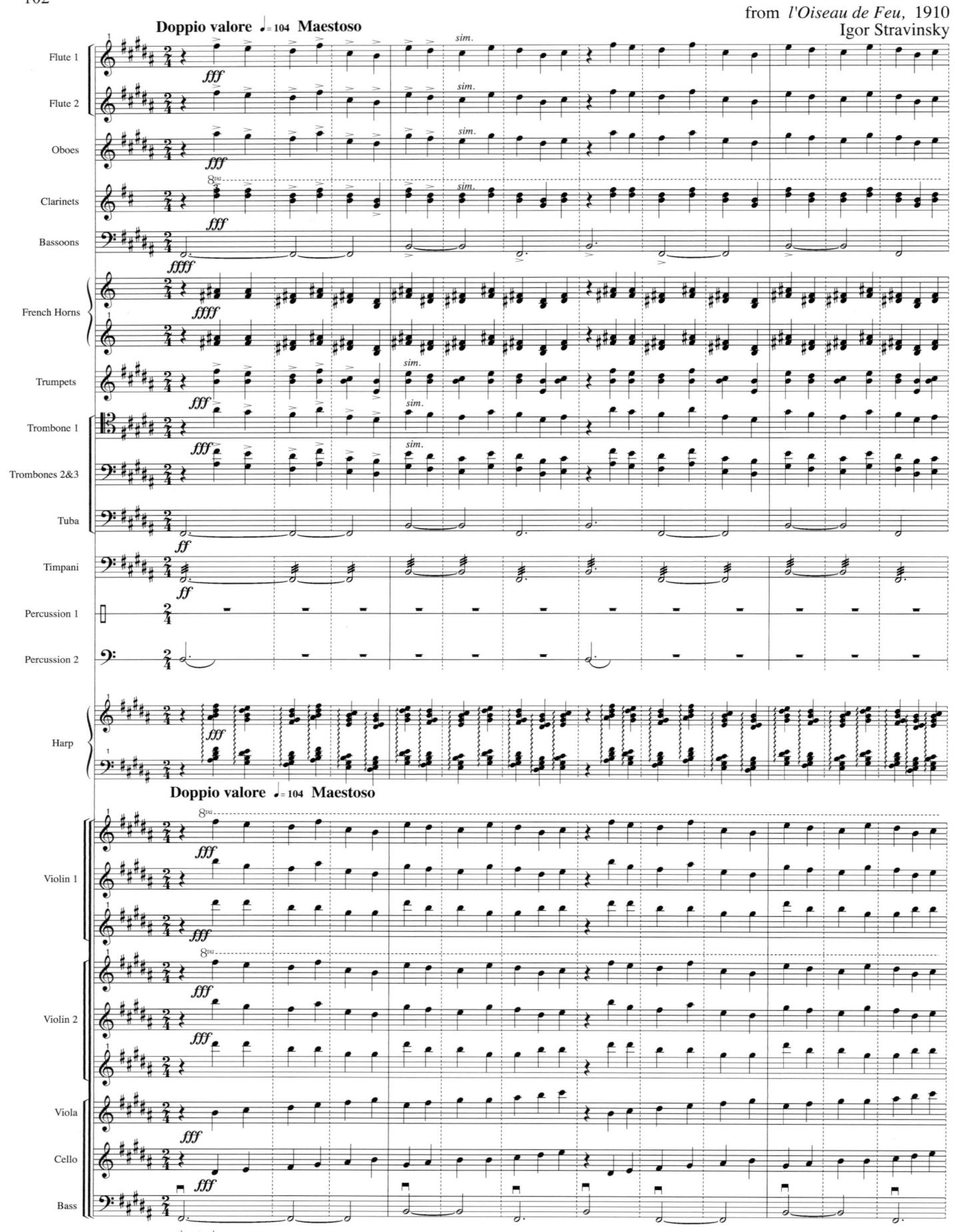

(Open Score #11, cont'd)

from *Elijah*
Felix Mendelssohn

12

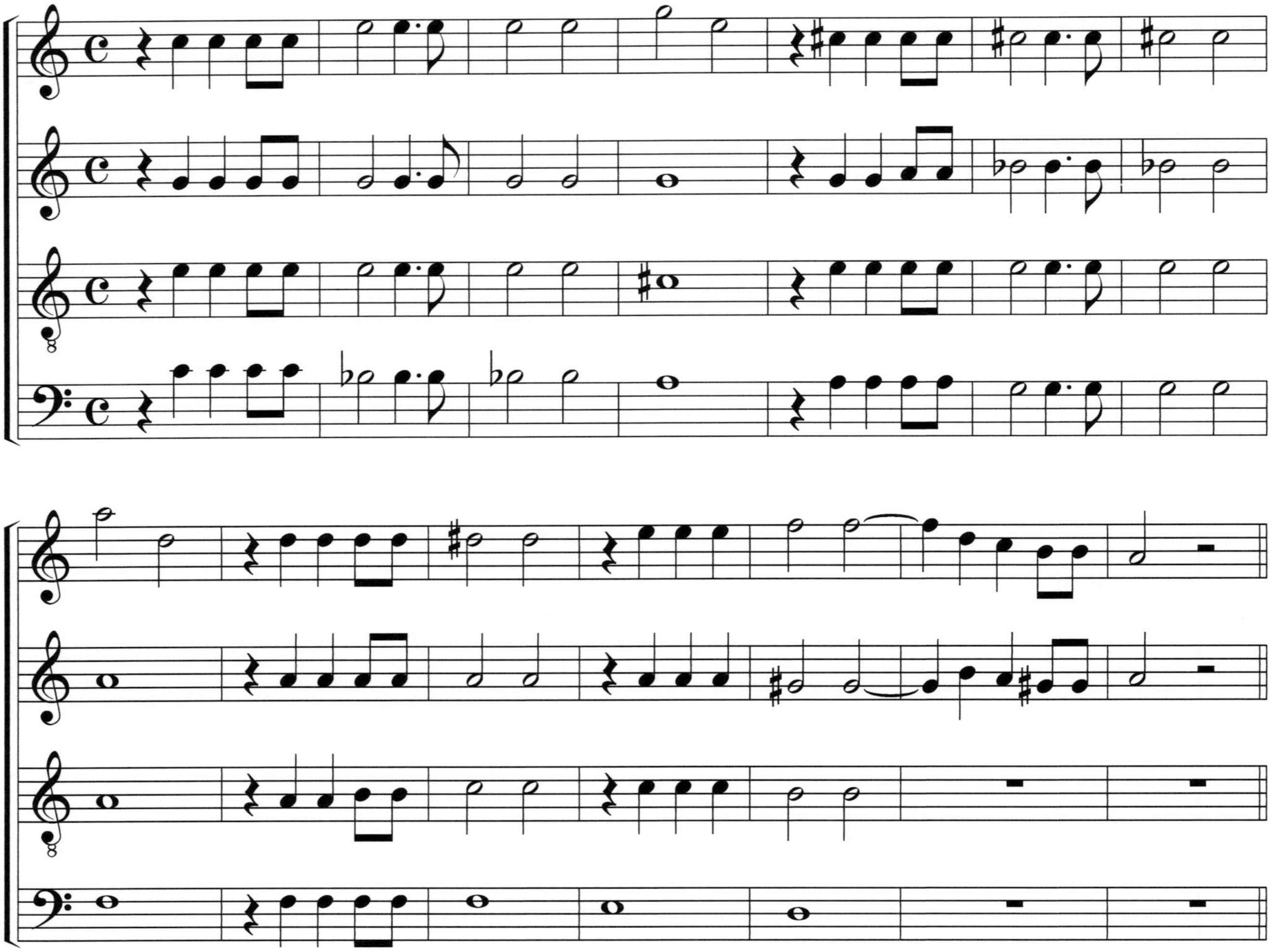

from *Gloria*
Antonio Vivaldi

13

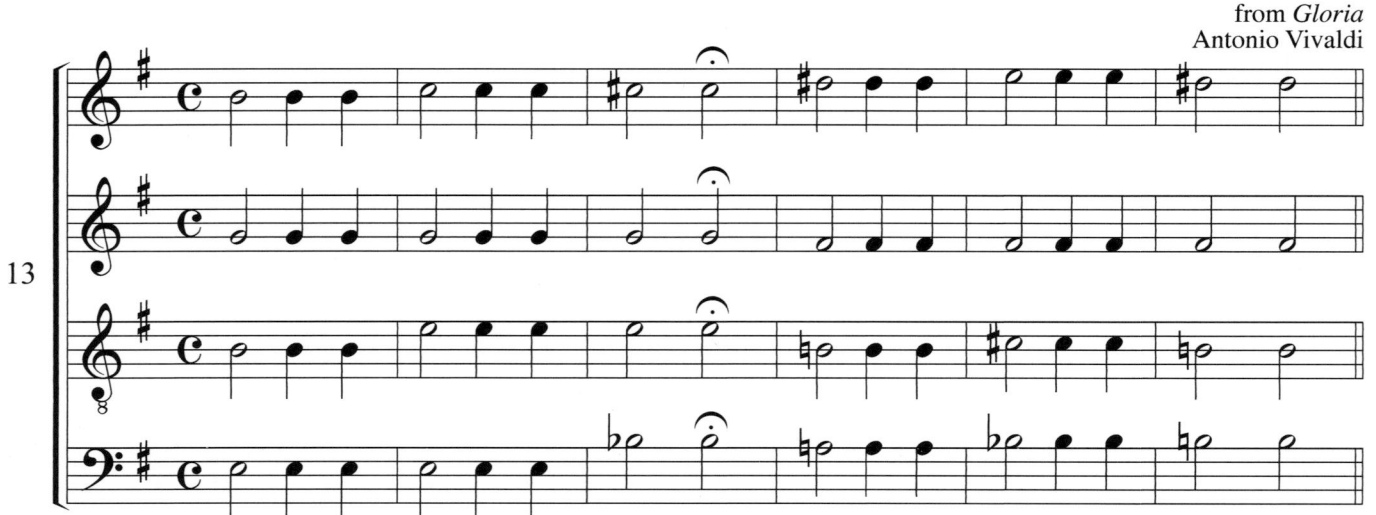

String Quartet in D Minor
Franz Schubert

Notturno, K. 436
W. A. Mozart

Franz Schubert

Jesu, Joy of Man's Desiring
J. S. Bach

17

G. Palestrina

18

Music © 2001 by Smith Creek Music, Nashville, TN 37214. All rights reserved. www.smithcreekmusic.com

108

from *Requiem*
W. A. Mozart

19

RETROSPECT
Wm. Billings

20

Music © 2001 by Smith Creek Music, Nashville, TN 37214. All rights reserved. www.smithcreekmusic.com

109

DUNDEE
Scottish Psalter

21

from *Messiah*
G. F. Handel

22

Music © 2001 by Smith Creek Music, Nashville, TN 37214. All rights reserved. www.smithcreekmusic.com

LEONI
Traditional Hebrew Melody

23

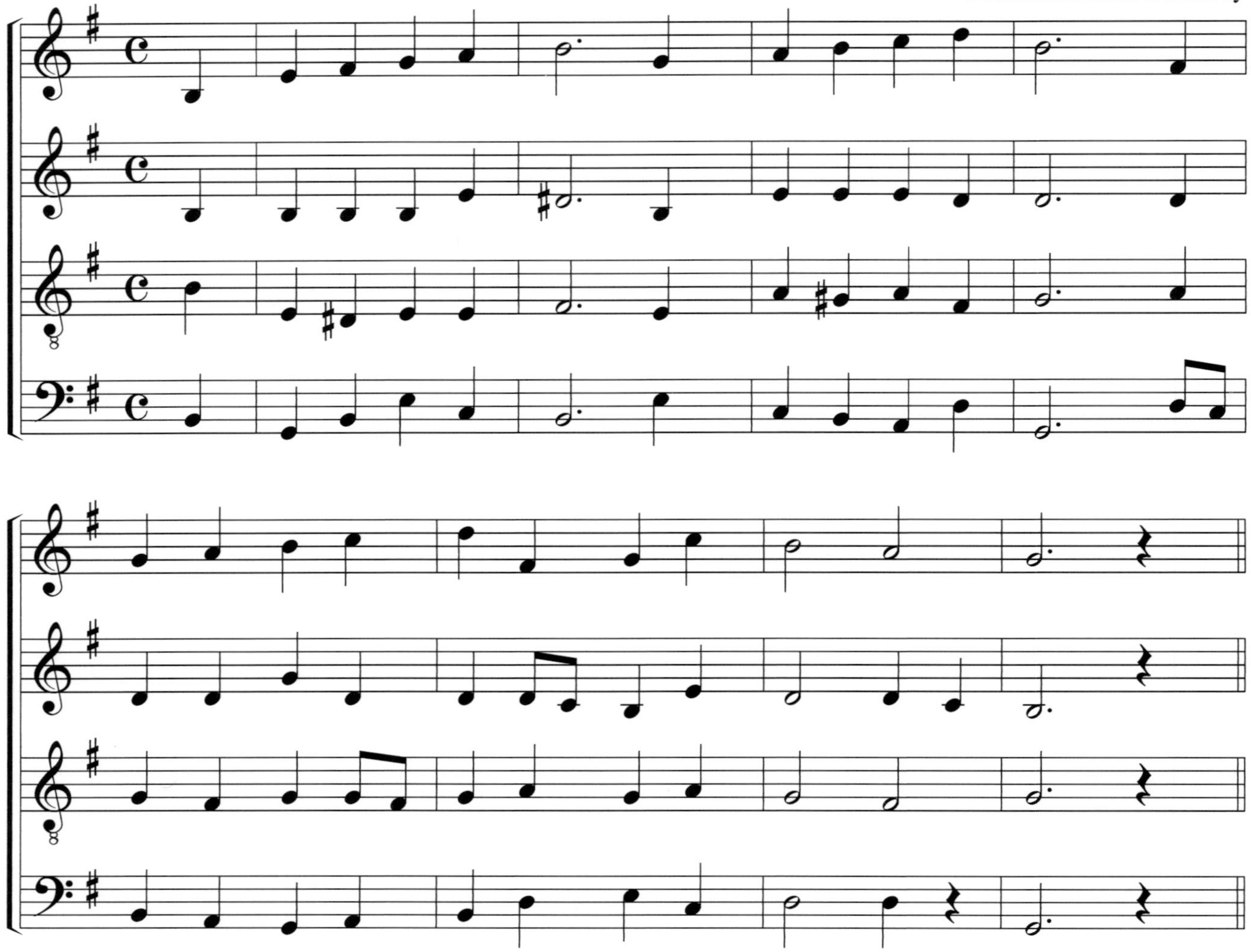

CHRIST LAG IN TODESBANDEN
Harmonized by J. S. Bach

24

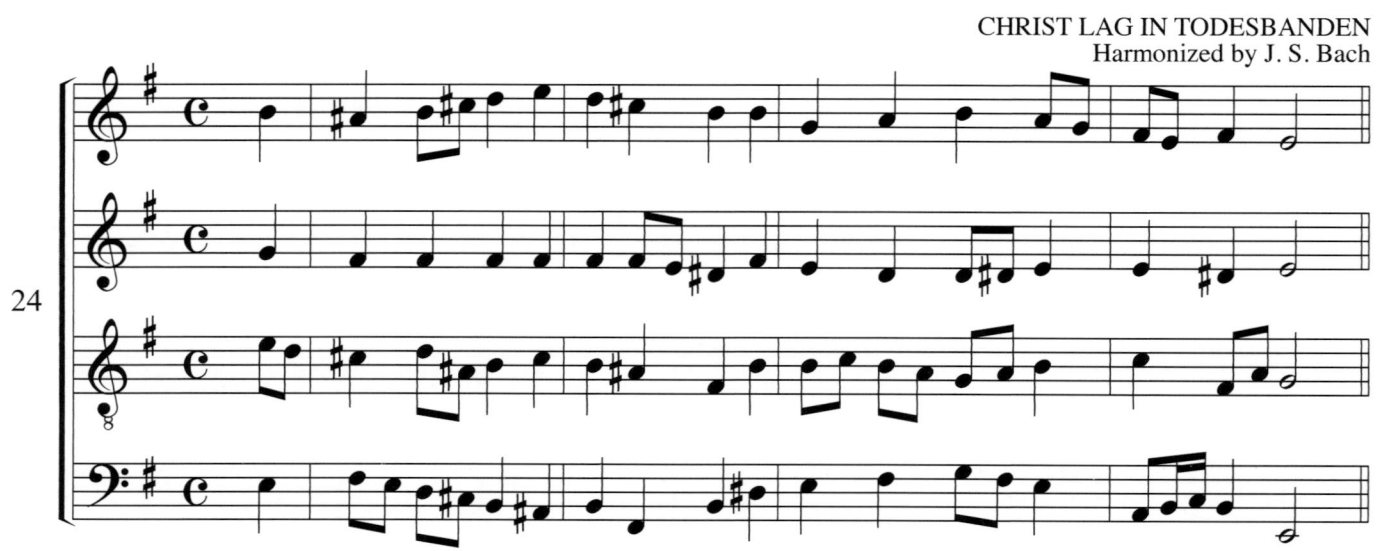

AVE VIRGO VIRGINUM
Leisentritt's, *Gesangbuch*

25

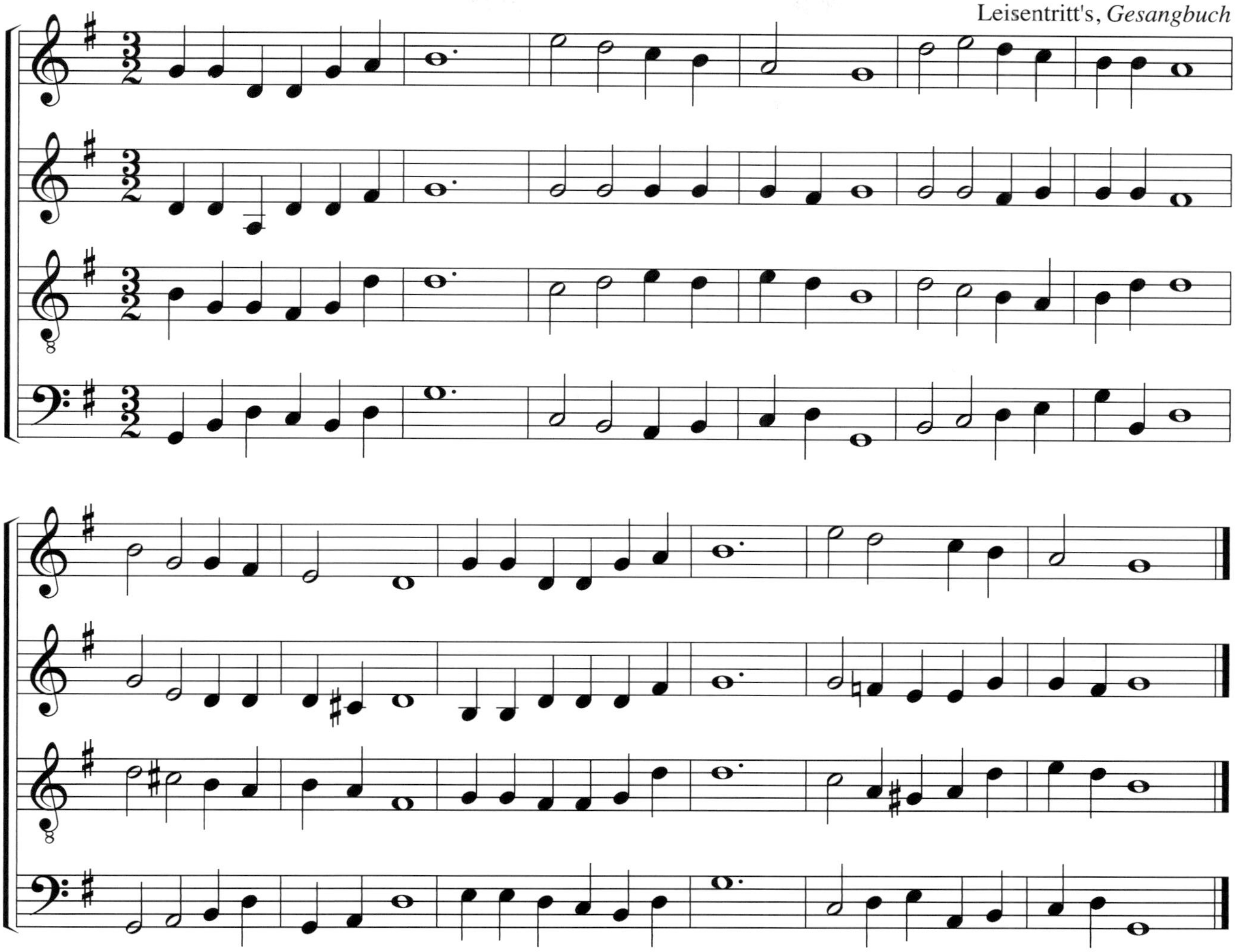

PASSION CHORALE
Harmonized by J. S. Bach

26

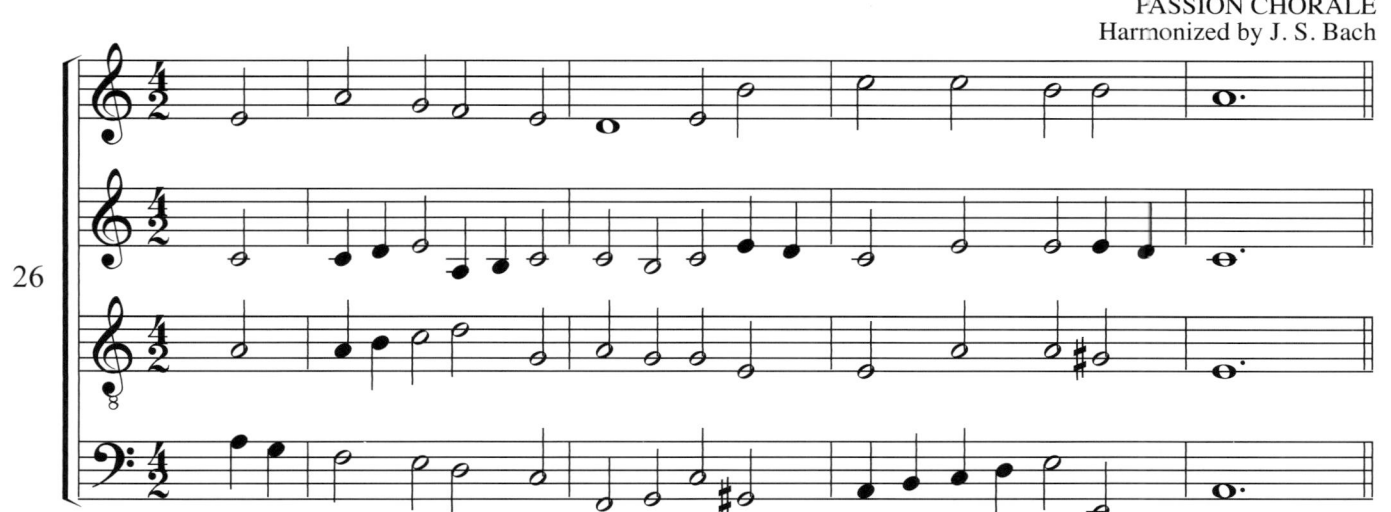

Scales

All major and minor scales can be divided into 3 "groups" according to their fingering patterns. Each group has its own characteristics and these are listed below. It is recommended that the student memorize each group of scales along with their characteristics and fingerings. Here are some general, introductory statements about scale fingerings.

1. In any scale (major or minor), the 4th finger in each hand only plays ONCE per octave. Consequently, the 4th finger always plays the SAME note. One way to think about scale fingerings is simply to know (memorize) the 4th finger note of each scale.

2. Fingering in scales is CONSECUTIVE, that is -- don't skip fingers. This is a common mistake, particularly skipping the 2nd finger.

Group I Scales: Those scales in which the thumbs always play together.

MAJOR KEYS	(thumb notes)	**MINOR KEYS**	(thumb notes)
D-Flat	F & C	b-flat	c & f
G-Flat	C-flat & F	e-flat	f & c-flat
B	B & E	b	b & e
F	F & C	f	f & c

Here are some characteristics which may help to play these scales using the correct fingering:

1. The thumbs of each hand always play together. In addition, each scale in this group has 2 thumb notes (see the above chart). The thumbs always play on the white notes — never on black notes.

2. For all the scales in this group, the 2nd and 3rd fingers of each hand play on or near the group of 2 black notes. The 2nd, 3rd, & 4th fingers of each hand play on or near the group of 3 black notes.

Group II Scales: Those scales which have the same fingering as C major.

Major: C D E G A
Minor: c d e g a

All four forms of the scales in Group 2 have the same fingering: major, natural minor, harmonic minor, and melodic minor. Listed below are some characteristics of Group 2 scales which may help you to play the scales using the correct fingering:

1. All scales in Group 2 have the same fingering as C Major:

   RH: 1, 2, 3, 1, 2, 3, 4, 1, 2, 3, 1, 2, 3, 4, 5
   LH: 5, 4, 3, 2, 1, 3, 2, 1, 4, 3, 2, 1, 3, 2, 1

2. 3rd fingers in each hand play together.
3. Right hand 4th finger plays only the 7th degree of the scale.
4. Left hand 4th finger plays only the 2nd degree of the scale.
5. The thumbs play together only on the tonic note.

Group III Scales: All other scales. This is more than just a "catch-all" group because the scales in this group DO have several common characteristics. Here are some broad statements about the scales in this group:

1. There are 3 major scales and 3 minor scales.
2. The LH fingering is THE SAME in all the scales in this group, both MAJOR and MINOR.

   LH: 3, 2, 1, 4, 3, 2, 1, 3, 2, 1, 4, 3, 2, 1, 3

   Notice that the LH starts on the THIRD finger and then crosses over to the FOURTH finger.
   To help you remember this think: 4th finger plays the 4th scale degree.

   A common mistake is to start on the SECOND finger in order to make the thumbs play together.
   The THUMBS DO NOT play together all the time in this group.

5. For the MAJOR scales, and for A-flat (g-sharp) minor, the RH 4th finger always plays the note B-flat.
6. For the MINOR scales, the 3rd fingers (both hands) always play together.
7. Except for F-sharp minor, the 4th fingers ALWAYS play on BLACK notes and not on white notes.*

MAJOR	**MINOR**
B-flat	c-sharp
E-flat	f-sharp*
A-flat	a-flat

   Here is the fingering for the MINOR scales in this group:

   RH: 3, 4, 1, 2, 3, 1, 2, 3, 4, 1, 2, 3, 1, 2, 3
   LH: 3, 2, 1, 4, 3, 2, 1, 3, 2, 1, 4, 3, 2, 1, 3

---

* The fingering described here for F-sharp minor is an alternate fingering. Please get assistance from your instructor if you would like to use the traditional F-sharp minor fingering.

Group I Scales
(Thumbs play together)

All scales should be played from memory, 2 octaves ascending and descending in a steady tempo with correct fingering.

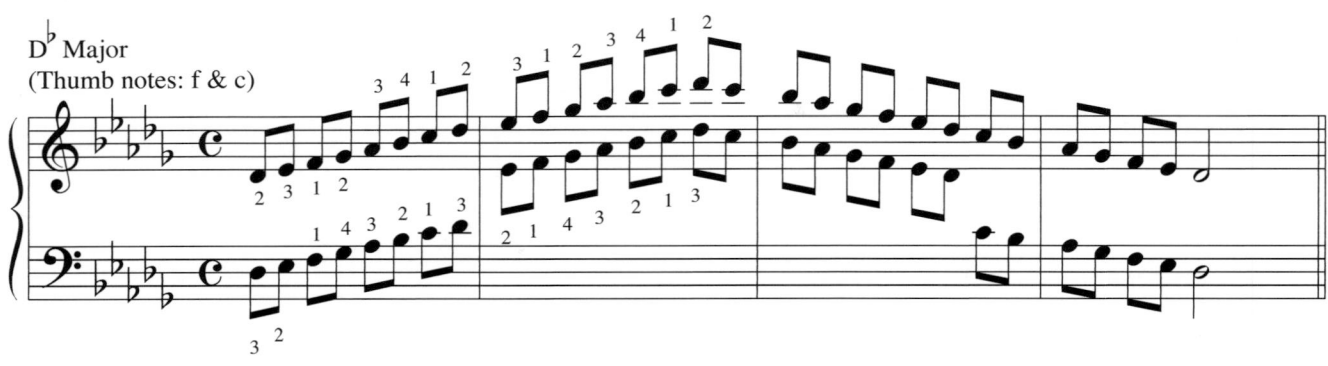

D♭ Major
(Thumb notes: f & c)

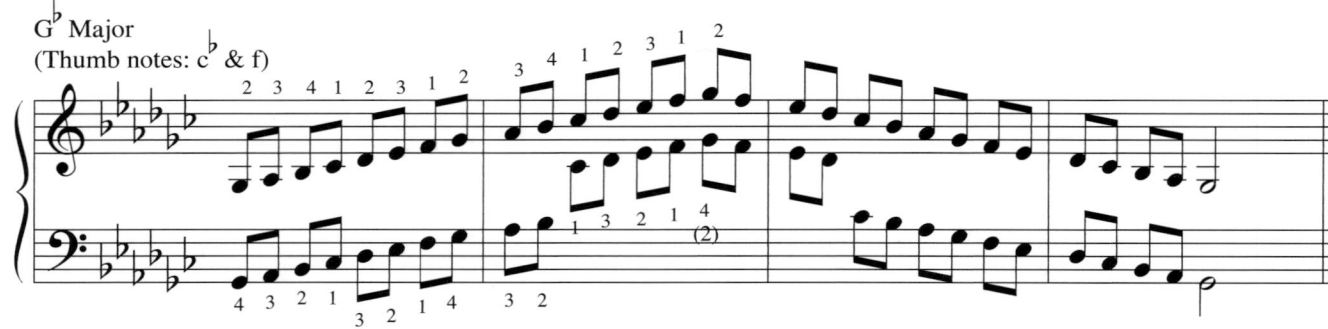

G♭ Major
(Thumb notes: c♭ & f)

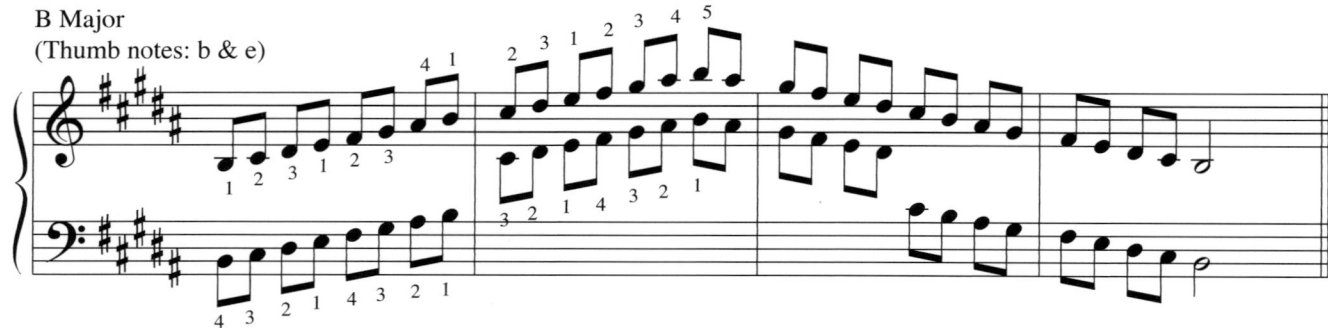

B Major
(Thumb notes: b & e)

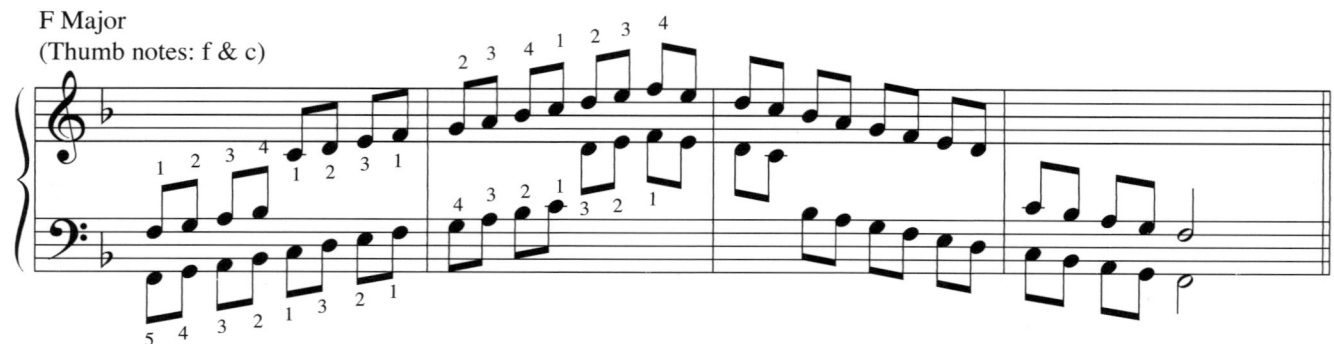

F Major
(Thumb notes: f & c)

Group I Scales, cont'd

B♭ harmonic minor
(Thumb notes: c & f)

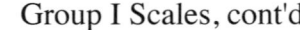

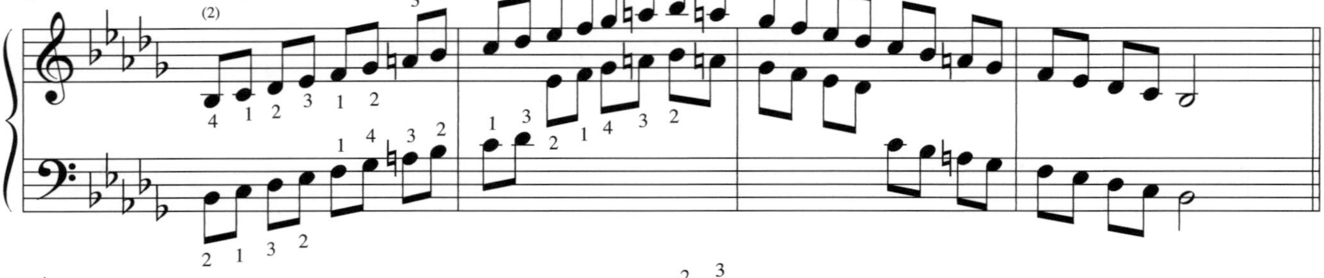

E♭ harmonic minor
(Thumb notes: f & c♭)

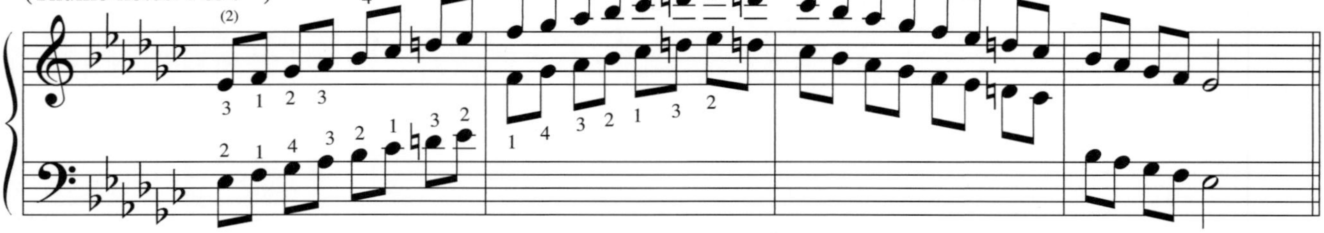

B harmonic minor
(Thumb notes: b & e)

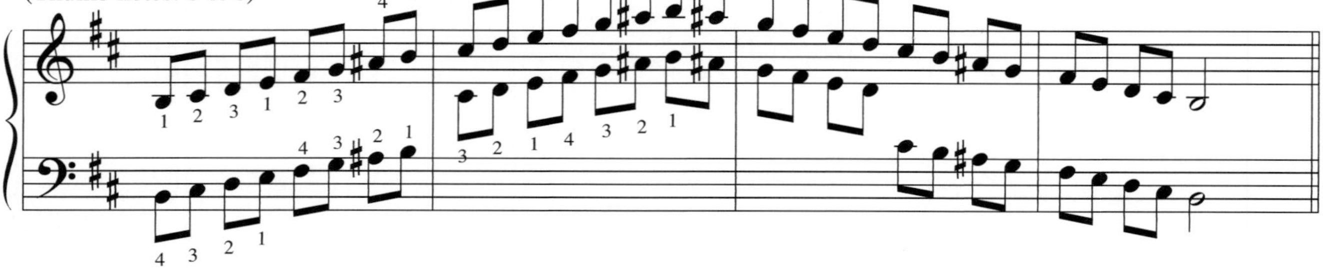

F harmonic minor
(Thumb notes: f & c)

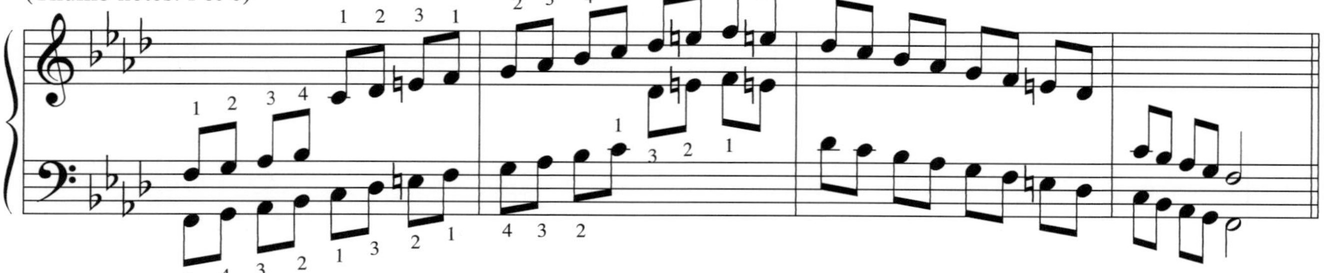

Group II Scales
(All scales in Group II have the same fingering as C Major.)

Group II Scales, cont'd

Group II Scales, cont'd

Group II Scales, cont'd

Group III Scales

Group III Scales, cont'd

Group I Arpeggios

All arpeggios should be played from memory, 2 octaves ascending and descending in a steady tempo with correct fingering. Unlike scales, there are several sets of fingering which different teachers use to teach arpeggios. You should use the fingering your instructor recommends. However, below is outlined a commonly used set of arpeggio fingering.

As with scales, arpeggios can be grouped according to specific fingering patterns. However, the groups of individual scales and arpeggios are not the same even though there are coincidently three groups of arpeggio fingerings.

GROUP I (fingered like C Major):   Right hand: 1 2 3 1 2 3 5
                                   Left hand: 5 4 2 1 4 2 1

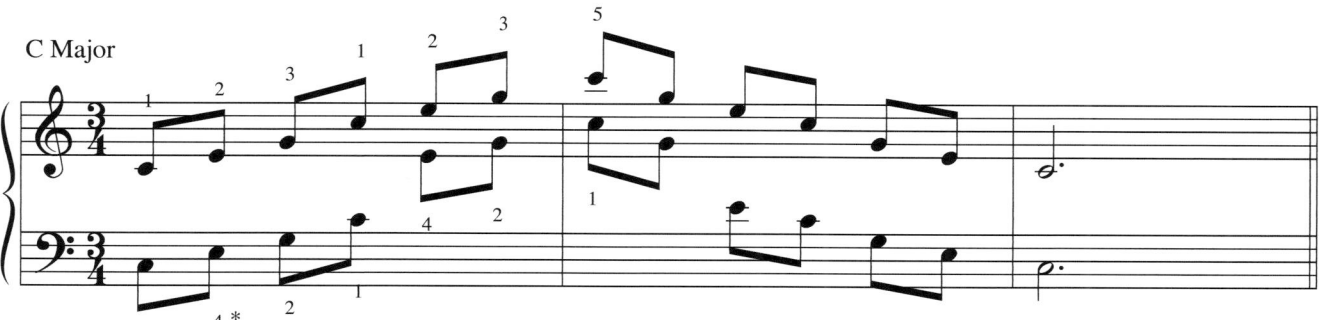

* Be sure to use the 4th finger in the left hand. Ask your teacher for an explanation of this fingering.

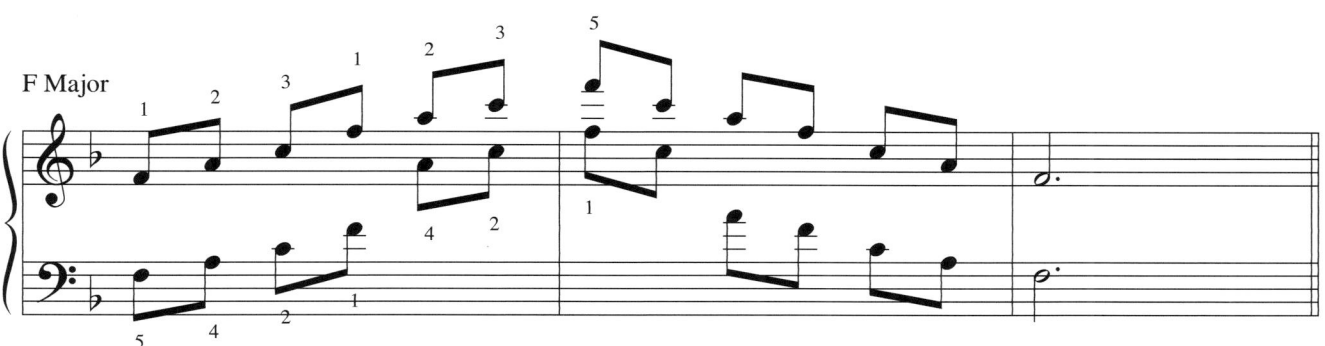

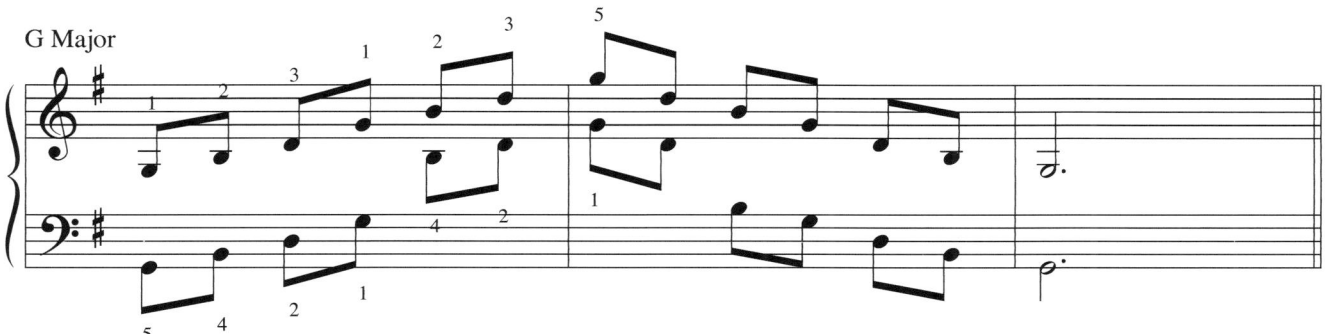

Group I Arpeggios, cont'd

Group I Arpeggios, cont'd

Group II Arpeggios

Group II arpeggios have the same fingering as Group I, except use the 3rd finger in the left hand instead of the 4th.

Group III Arpeggios

Group III arpeggios are sometimes called the "black key arpeggios" because they all start on a black key. All the arpeggios in this group have a mixture of black keys and white keys and the thumbs always play together on the first white key.

* The fingering in parentheses for B-flat major arpeggio is the traditional fingering. However thie alternate fingering beginning with the 2nd finger of the left hand is the one recommended in this series.

Group III Arpeggios, cont'd

Scale and Arpeggio Practice Log

Scales	1	2	3	4	5	6	7	8	9	10	11	12	13	14	15	16	17	18	19
D-flat																			
G-flat																			
B																			
F																			
B-flat minor																			
E-flat minor																			
B minor																			
F minor																			
C																			
D																			
E																			
G																			
A																			
C minor																			
D minor																			
E minor																			
G minor																			
A minor																			
B-flat																			
E-flat																			
A-flat																			
C-sharp minor																			
F-sharp minor																			
A-flat minor																			

Arpeggios	1	2	3	4	5	6	7	8	9	10	11	12	13	14	15	16	17	18	19
C																			
F																			
G																			
C minor																			
D minor																			
E minor																			
F minor																			
G minor																			
A minor																			
B minor																			
E-flat minor																			
D																			
E																			
A																			
B																			
G-flat																			
D-flat																			
E-flat																			
A-flat																			
B-flat																			
C-sharp minor																			
F-sharp minor																			
A-flat minor																			
B-flat minor																			

Exercises

Exercise #1 Ascending

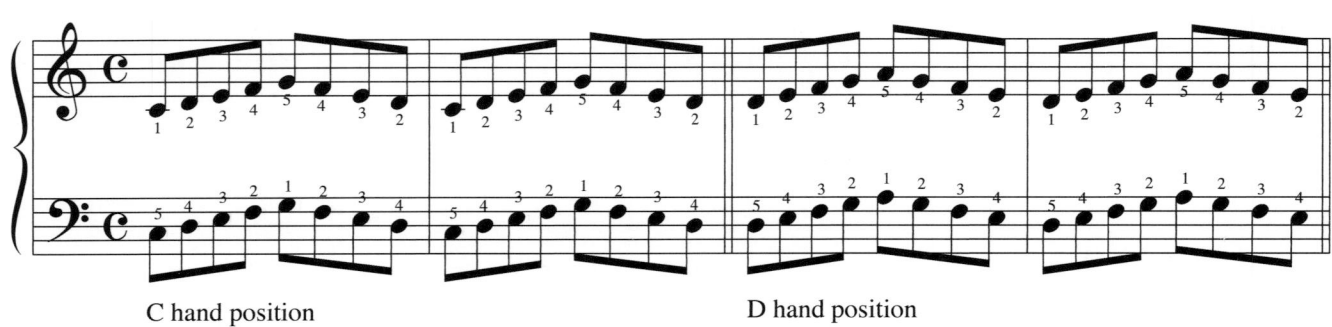

C hand position   D hand position

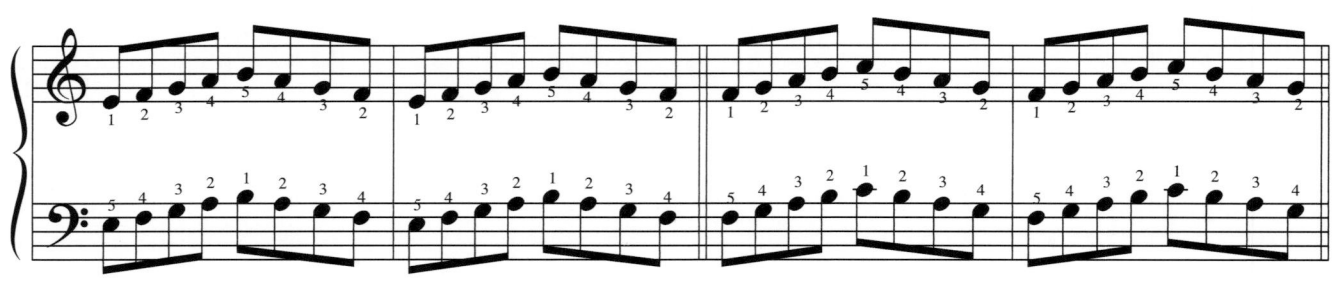

E hand position   F hand position

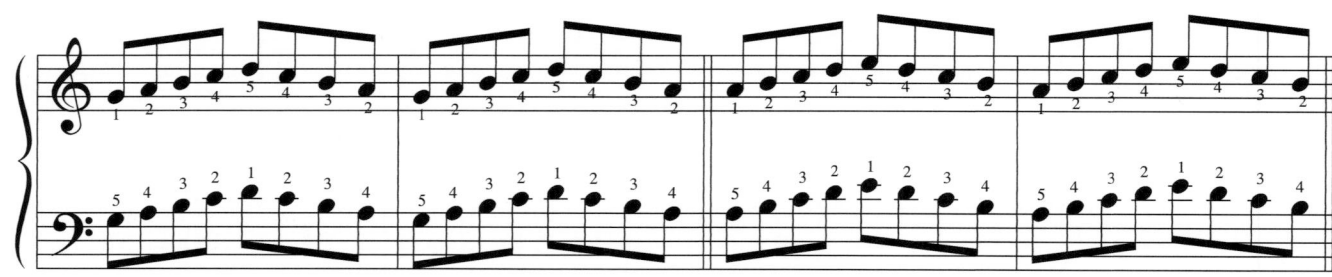

G hand position   A hand position

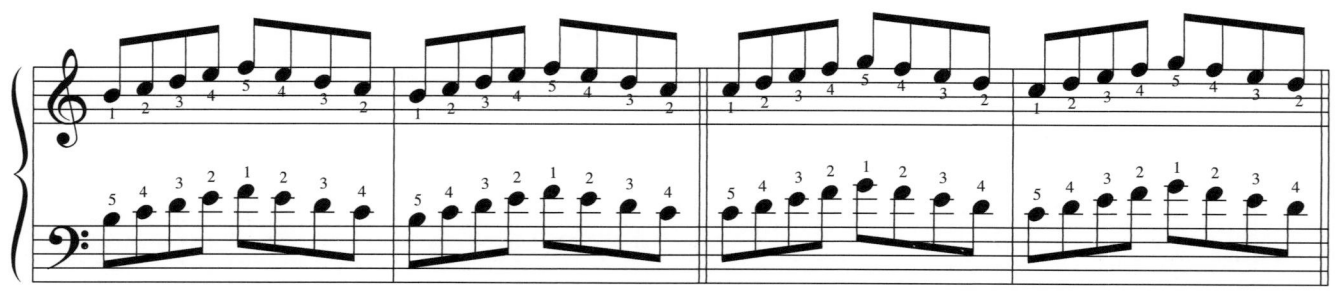

B hand position   C hand position

Exercise #1 Descending

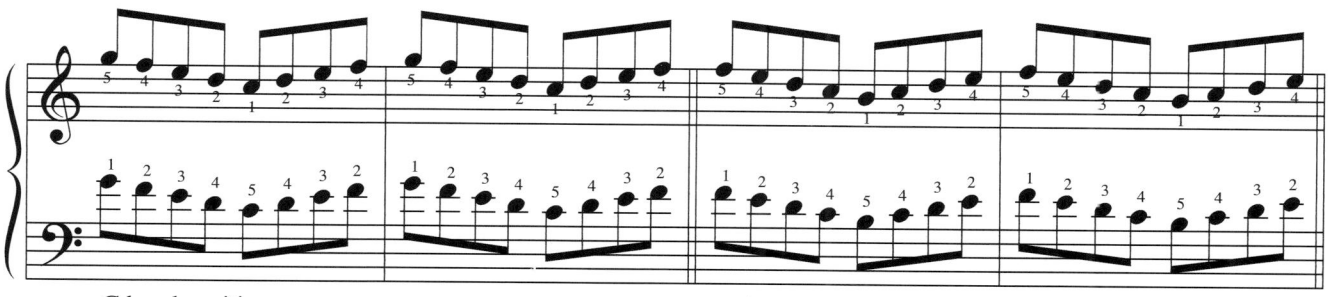

C hand position   B hand position

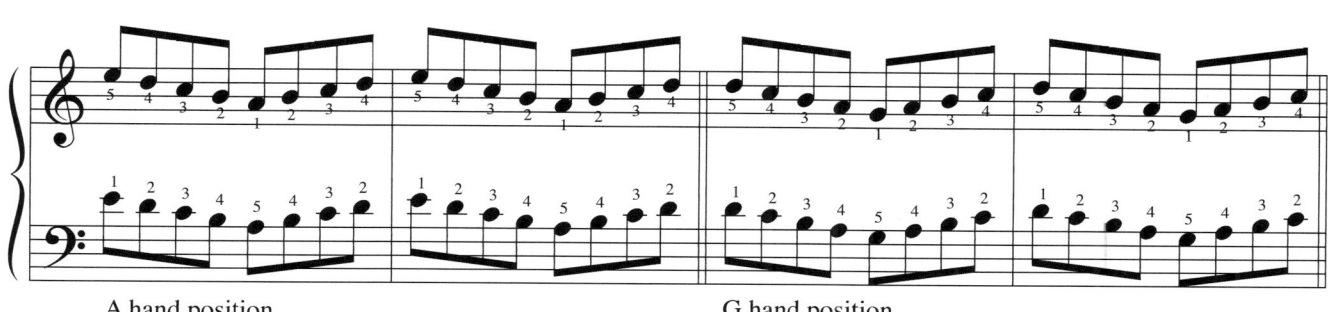

A hand position   G hand position

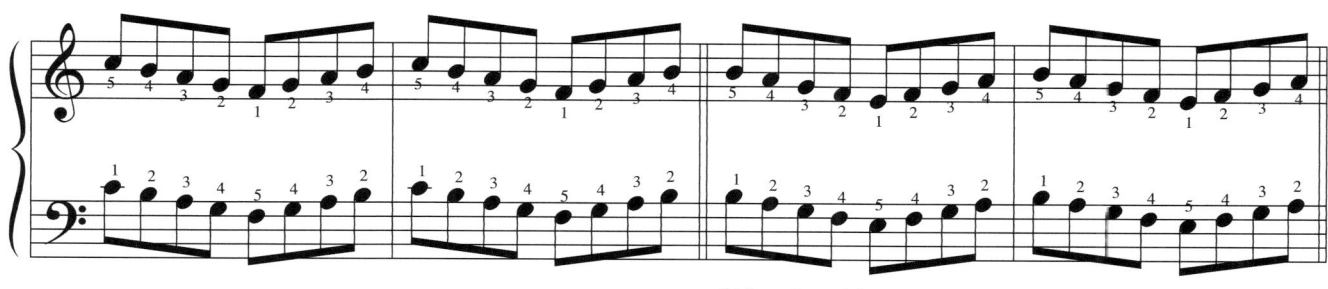

F hand position   E hand position

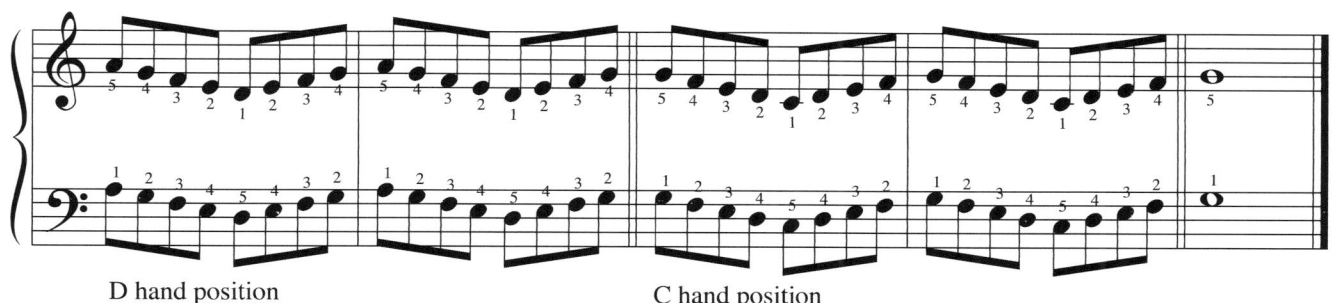

D hand position   C hand position

Exercise #2 Ascending

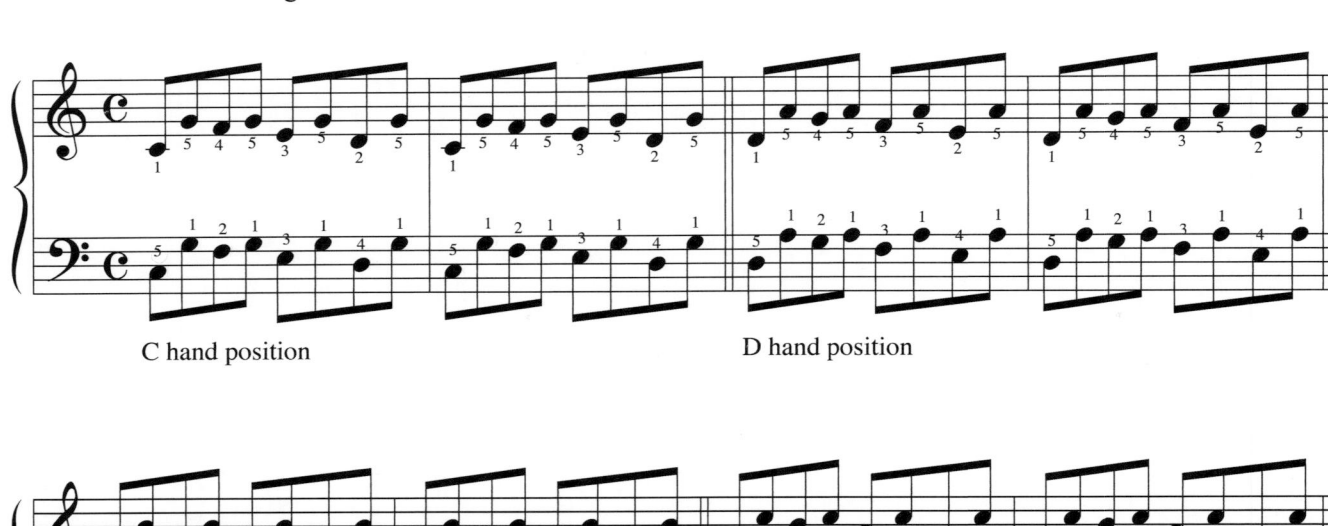

C hand position   D hand position

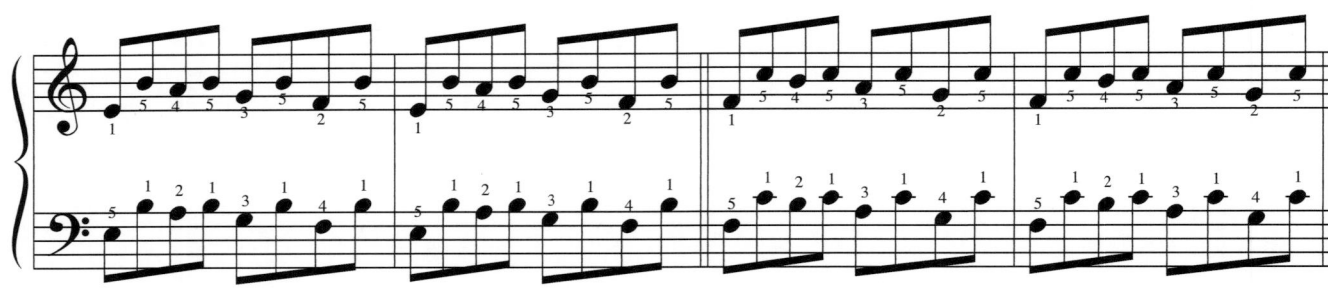

E hand position   F hand position

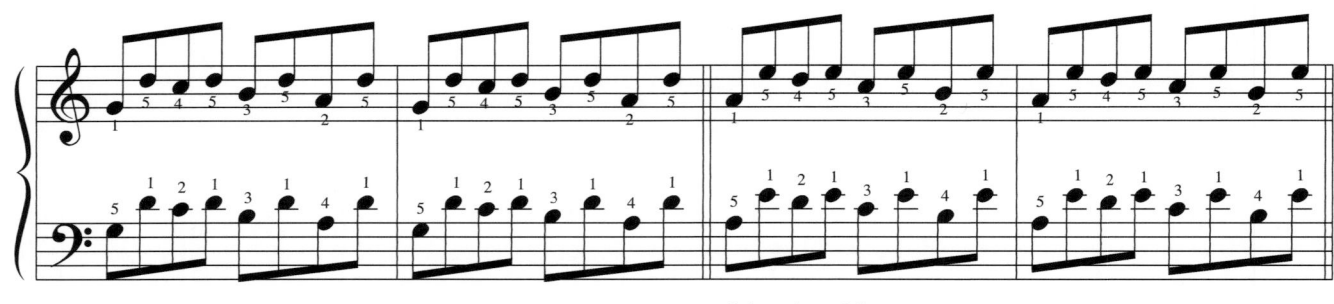

G hand position   A hand position

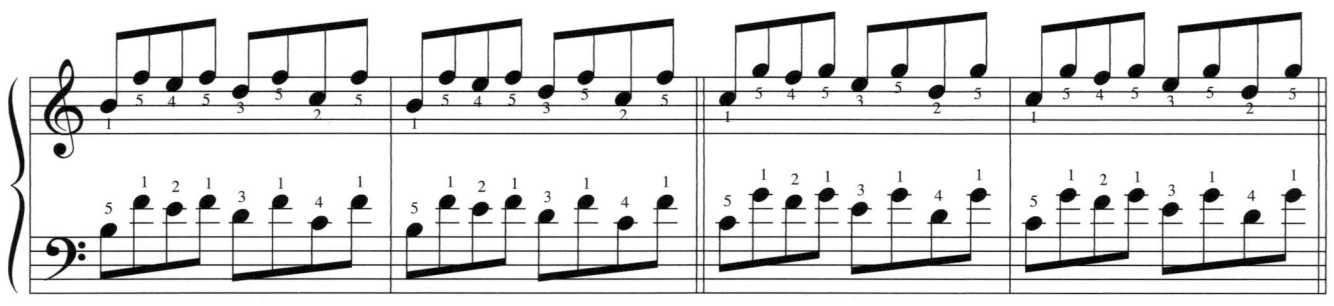

B hand position   C hand position

Exercise #2 Descending

C hand position — B hand position

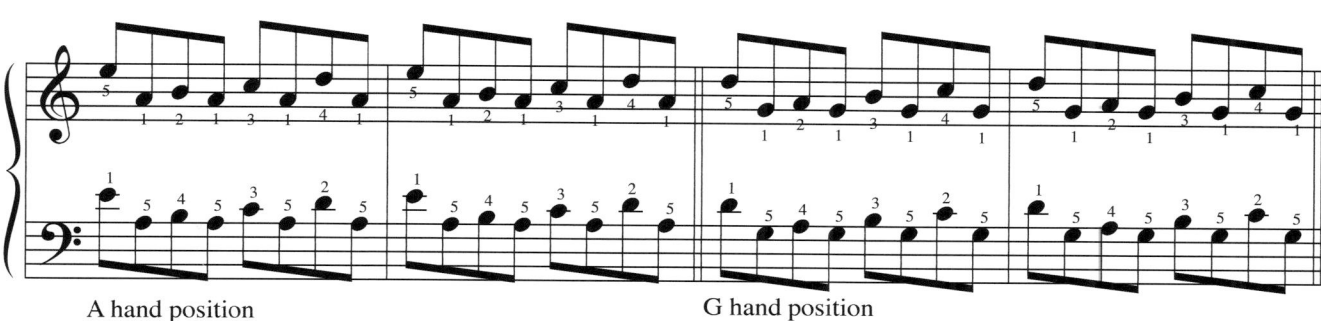

A hand position — G hand position

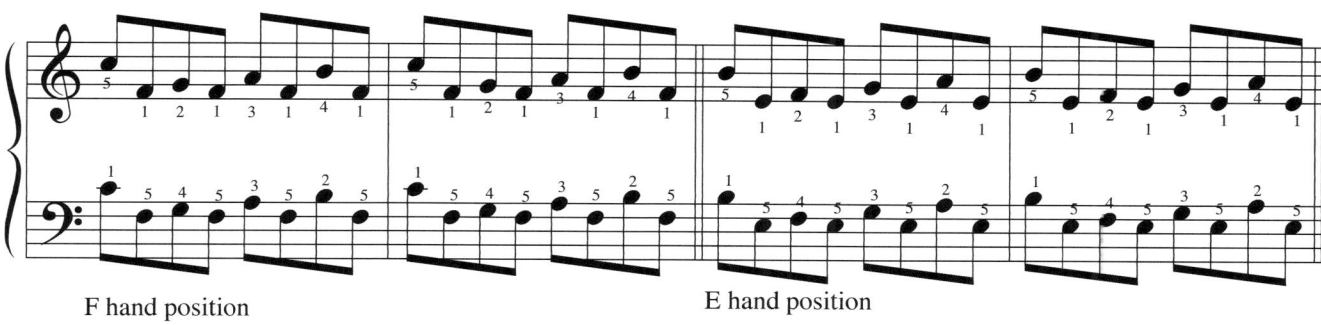

F hand position — E hand position

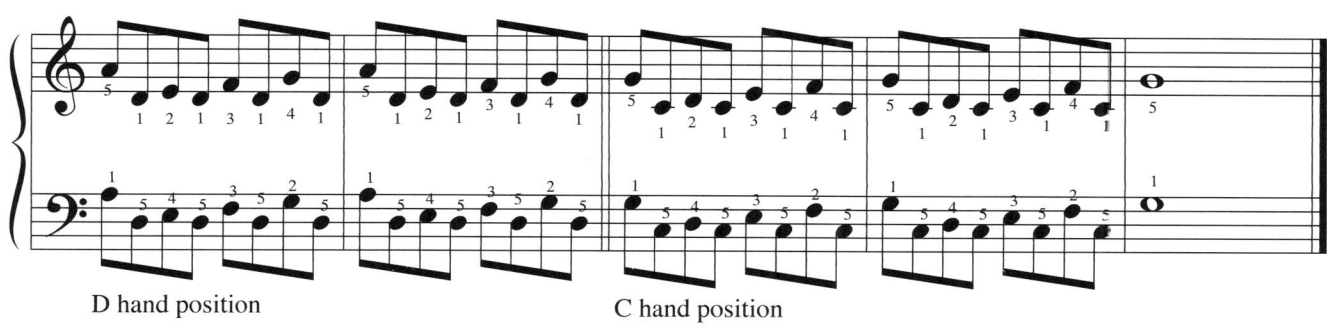

D hand position — C hand position

Exercise #3 Ascending

Exercise #3 Descending

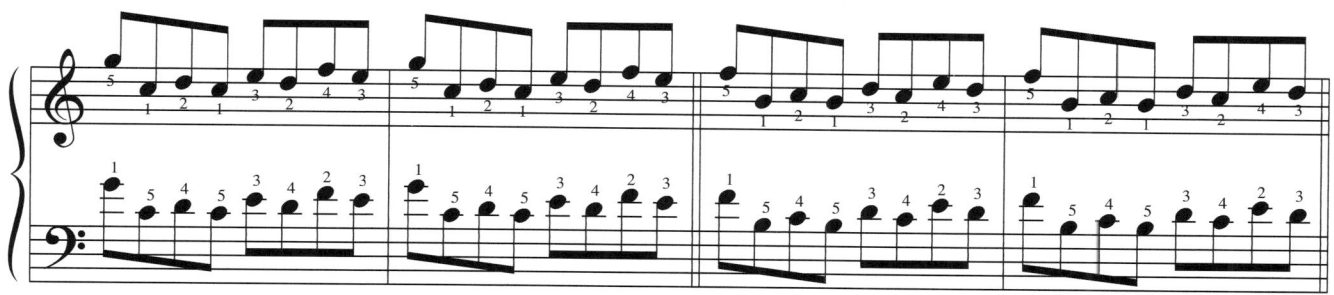

C hand position   B hand position

A hand position   G hand position

F hand position   E hand position

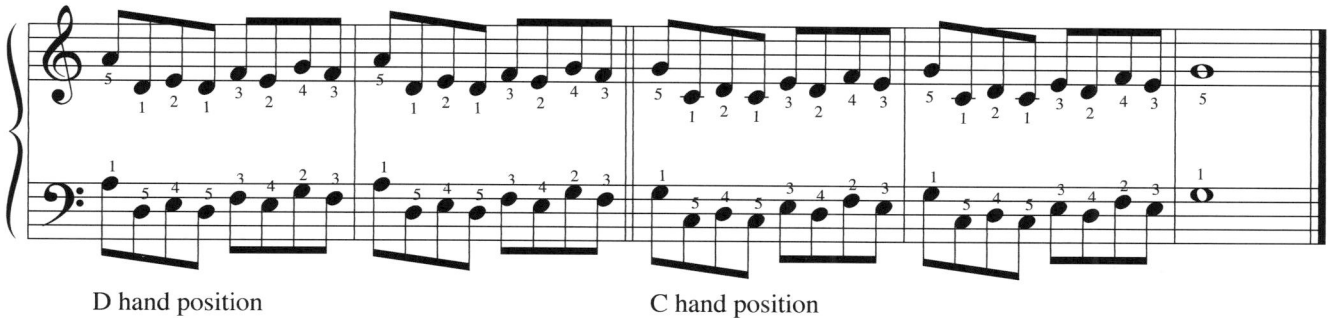

D hand position   C hand position

Exercise #4 Ascending

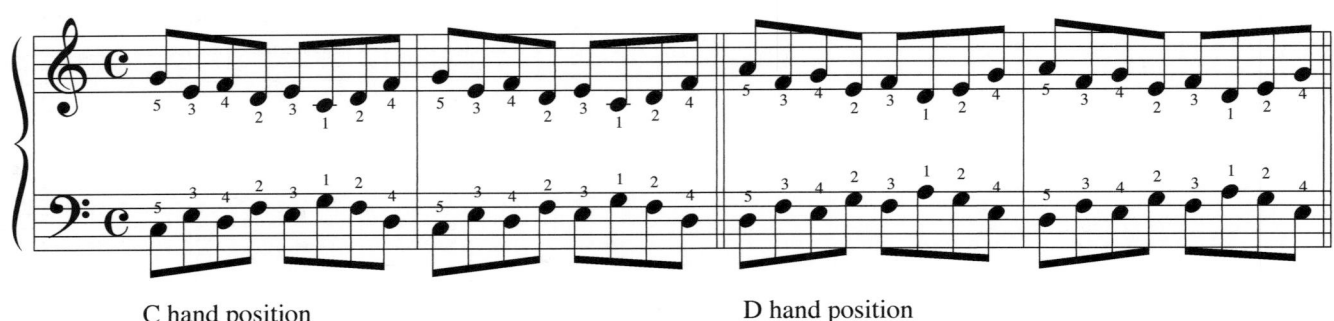

C hand positionD hand position

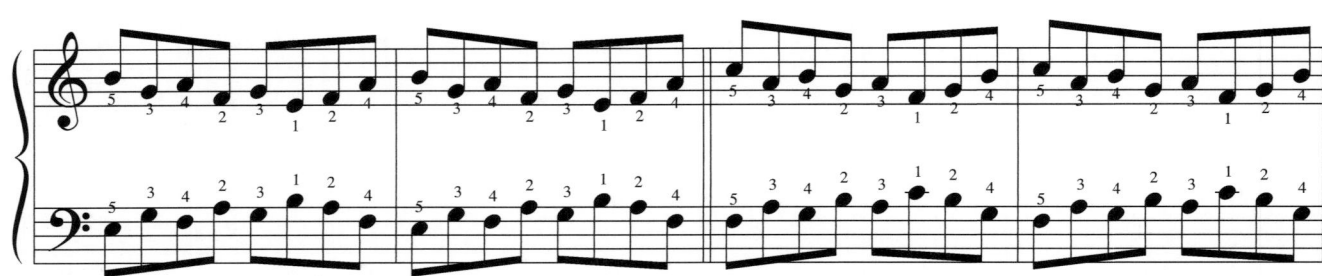

E hand positionF hand position

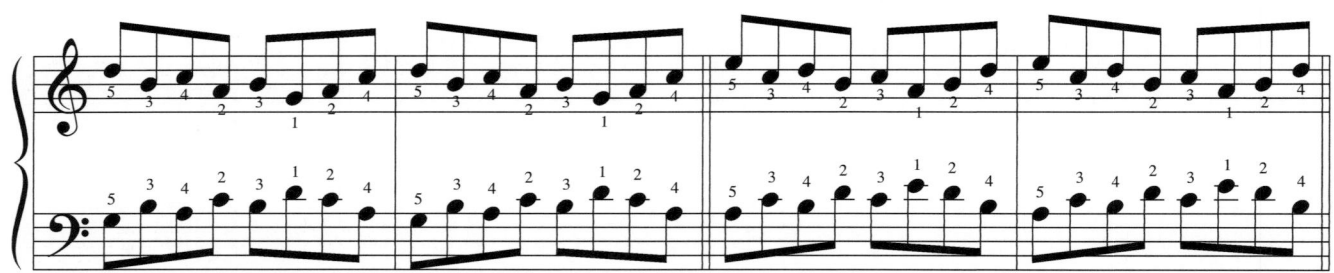

G hand positionA hand position

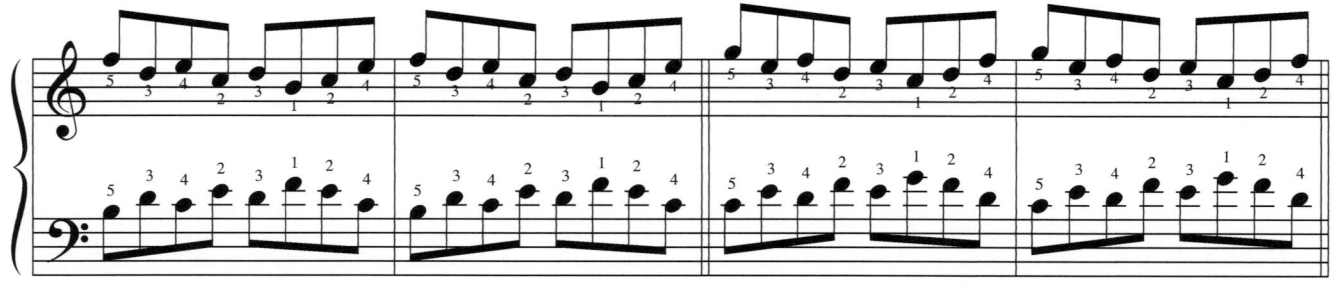

B hand positionC hand position

Exercise #4 Descending

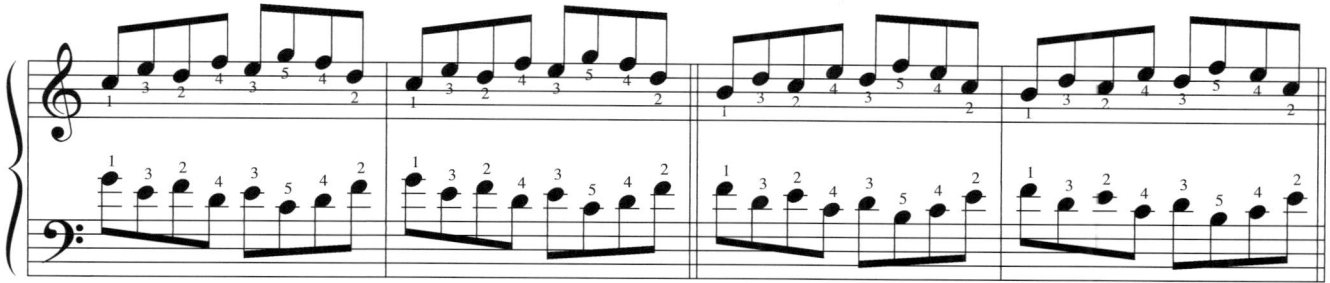

C hand position   B hand position

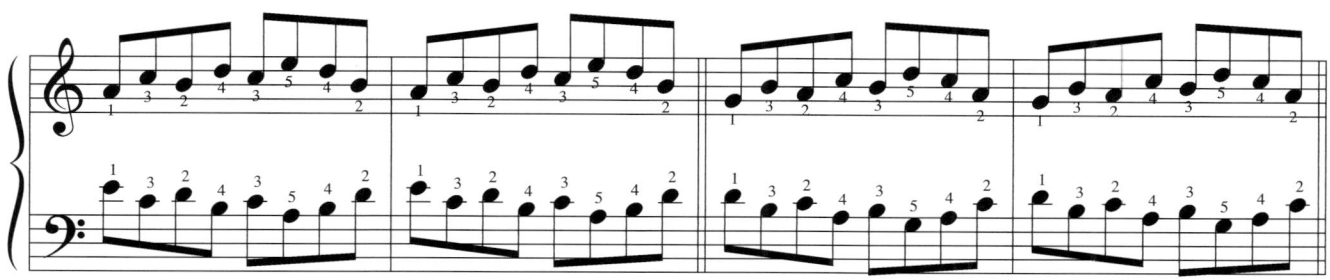

A hand position   G hand position

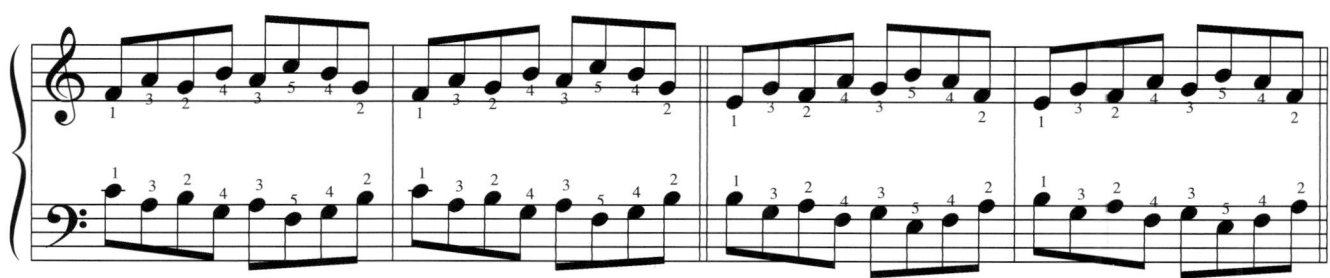

F hand position   E hand position

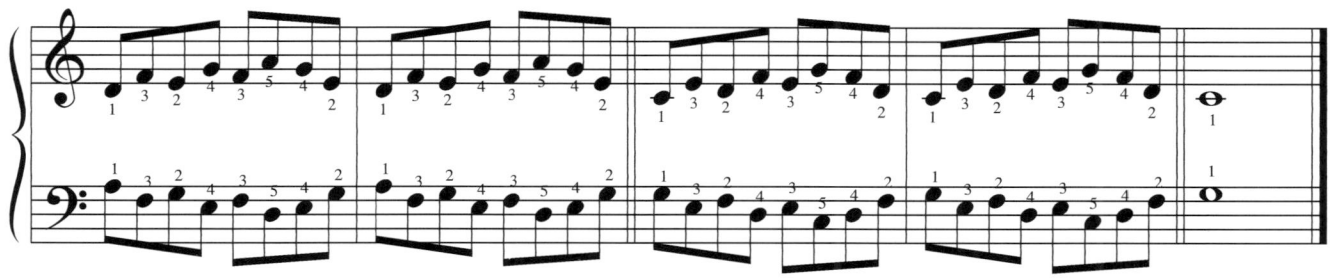

D hand position   C hand position

Exercise #5 Ascending

C hand position   D hand position

E hand position   F hand position

G hand position   A hand position

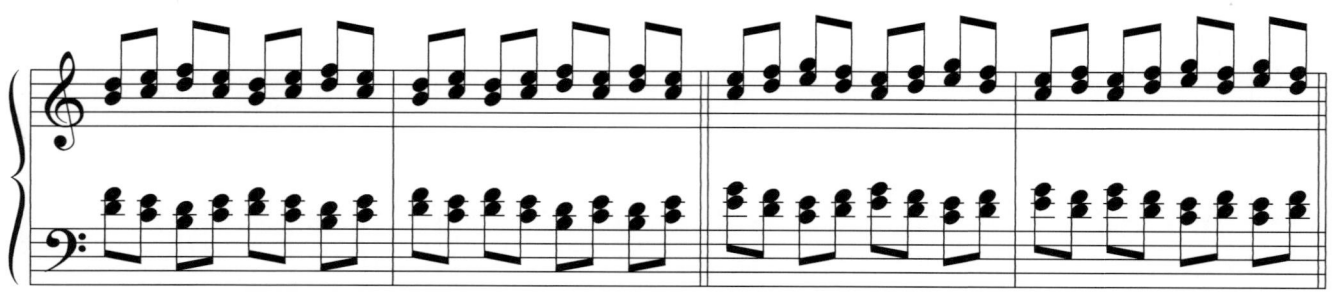

B hand position   C hand position

Exercise #5 Descending

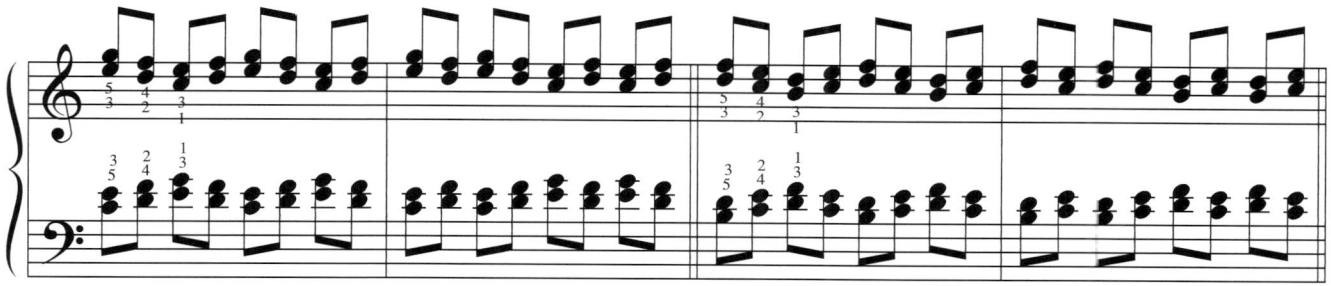

C hand position   B hand position

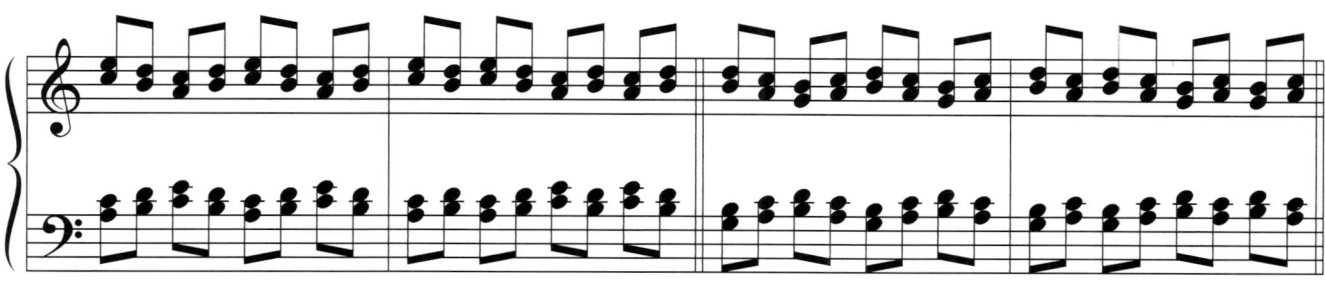

A hand position   G hand position

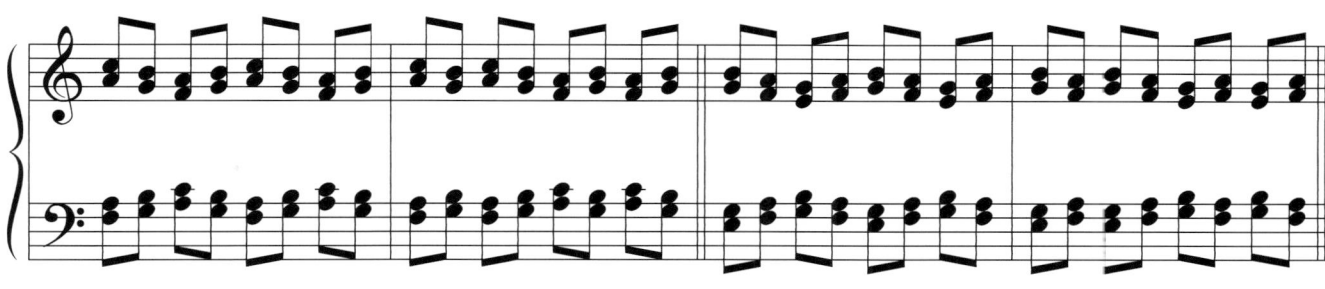

F hand position   E hand position

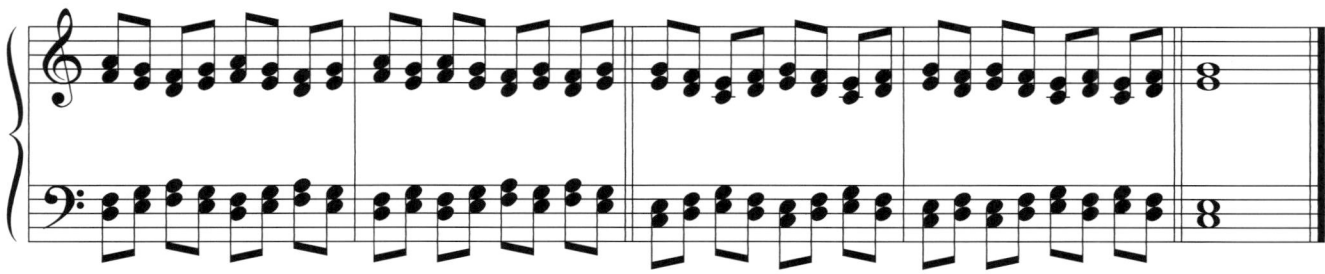

D hand position   C hand position

Exercise #6 Ascending

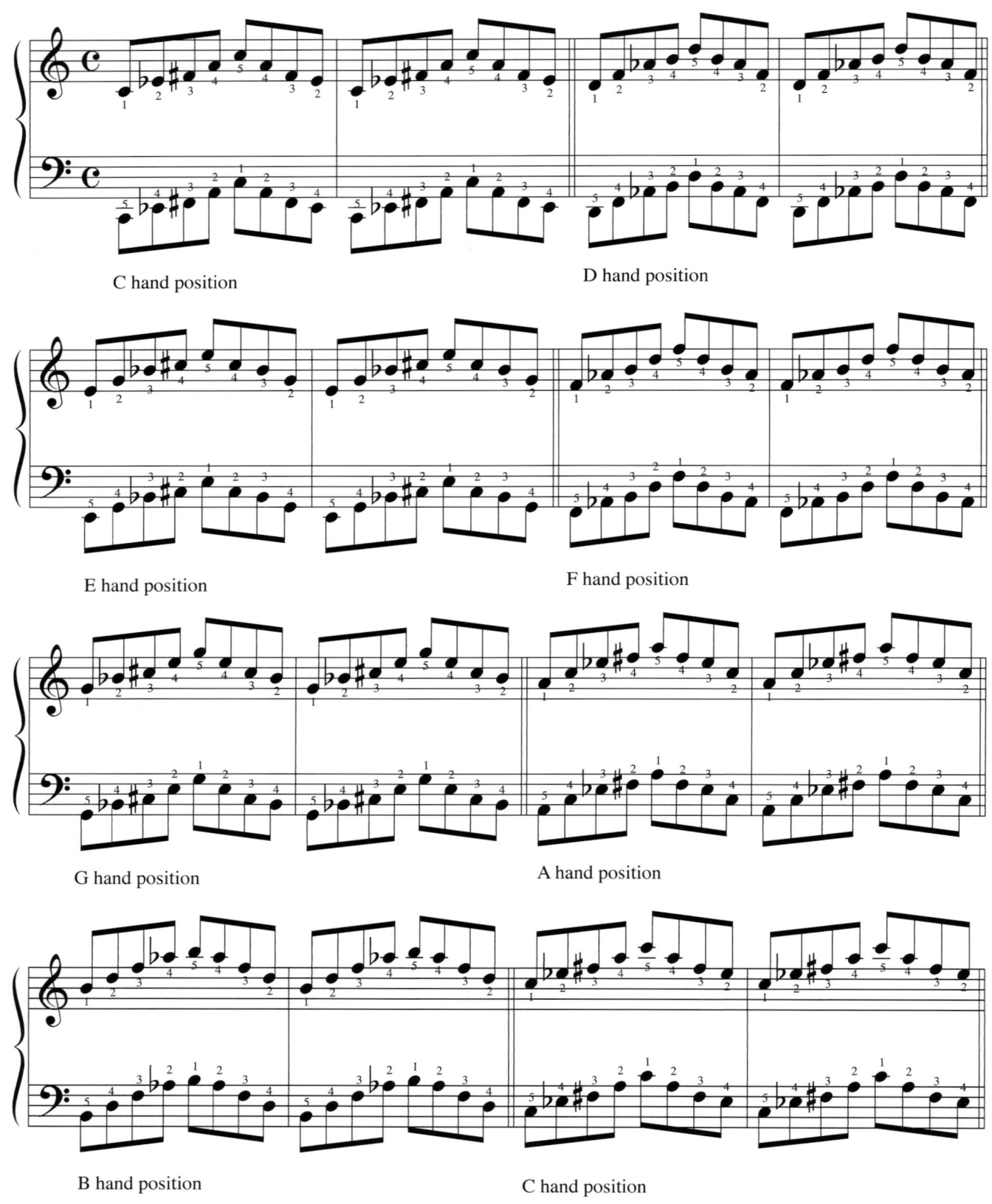

Exercise #6 Descending

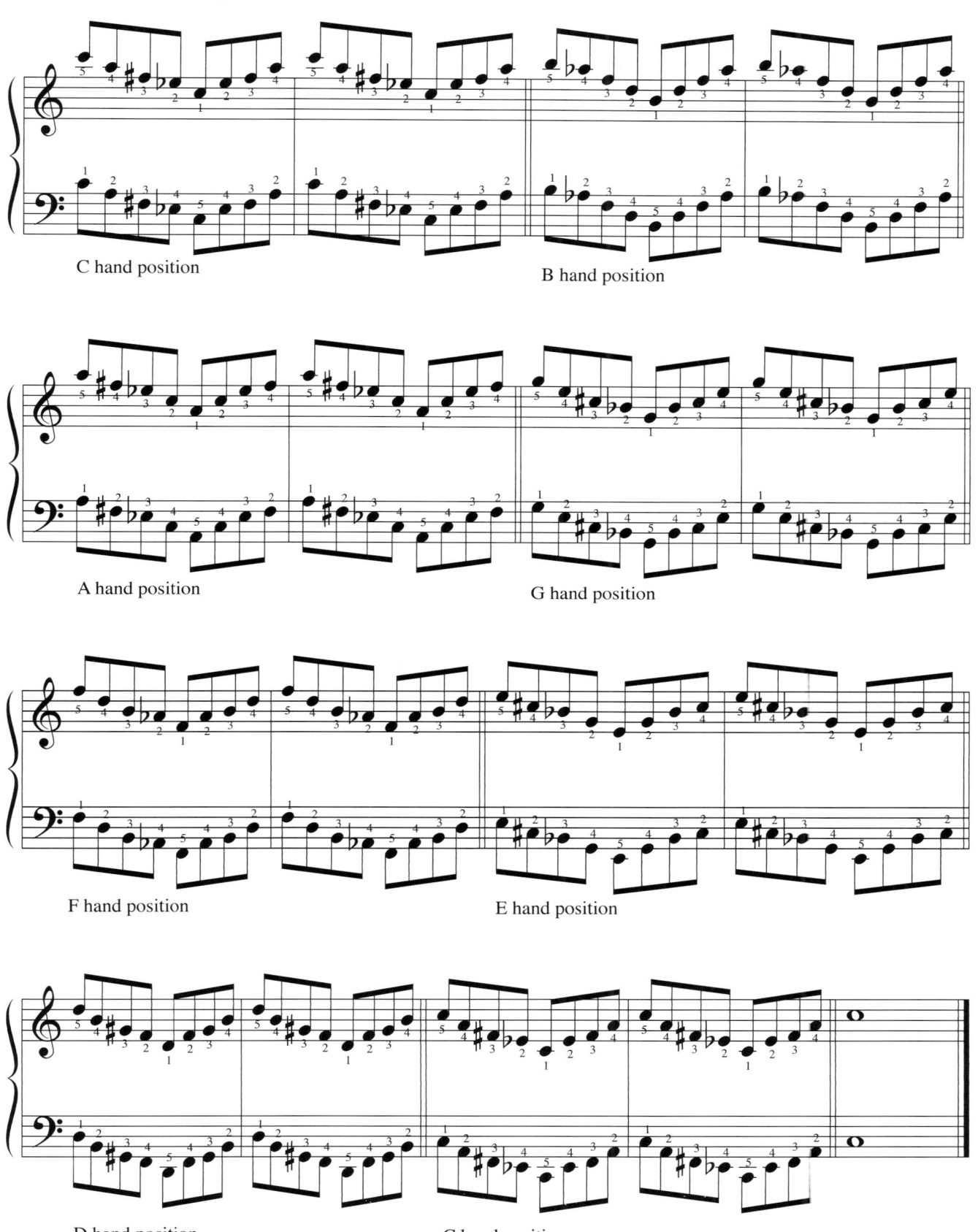

Exercise #7 Ascending

Exercise #7 Descending

Appendix 1: Triads in a Scale; Inversions of Triads

Root position triads: C Major

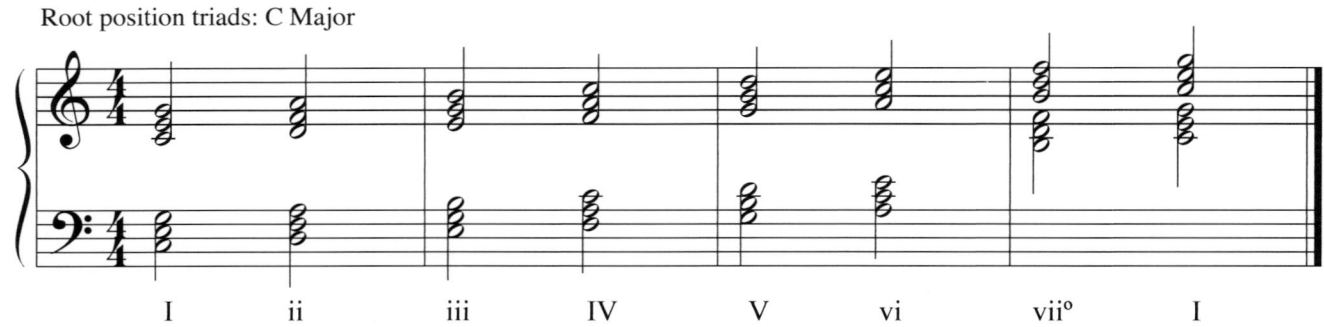

Inversions of primary triads: C Major

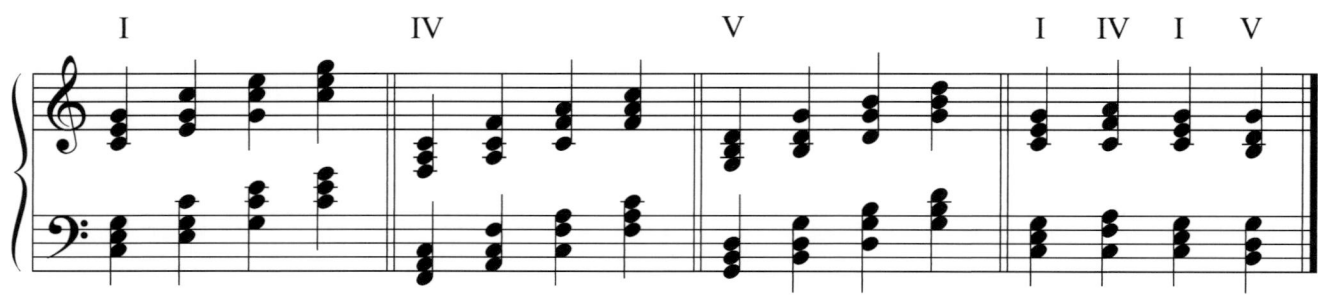

Root position triads: A minor

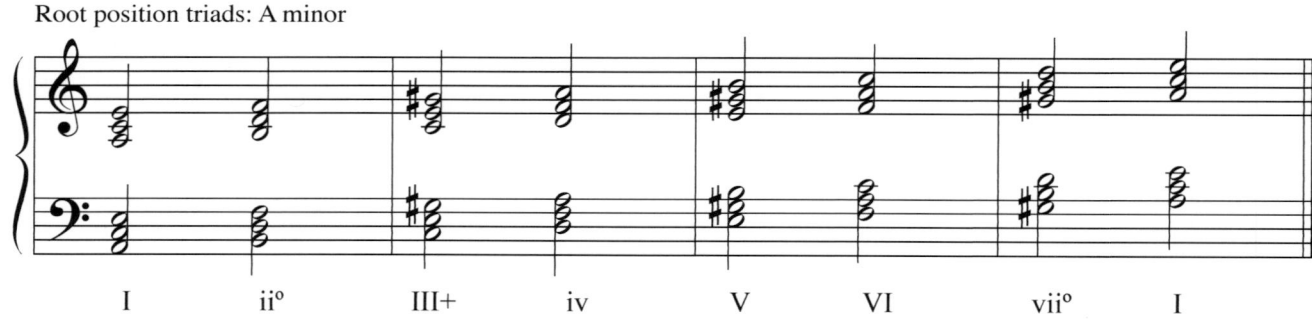

Inversions of primary triads: A minor

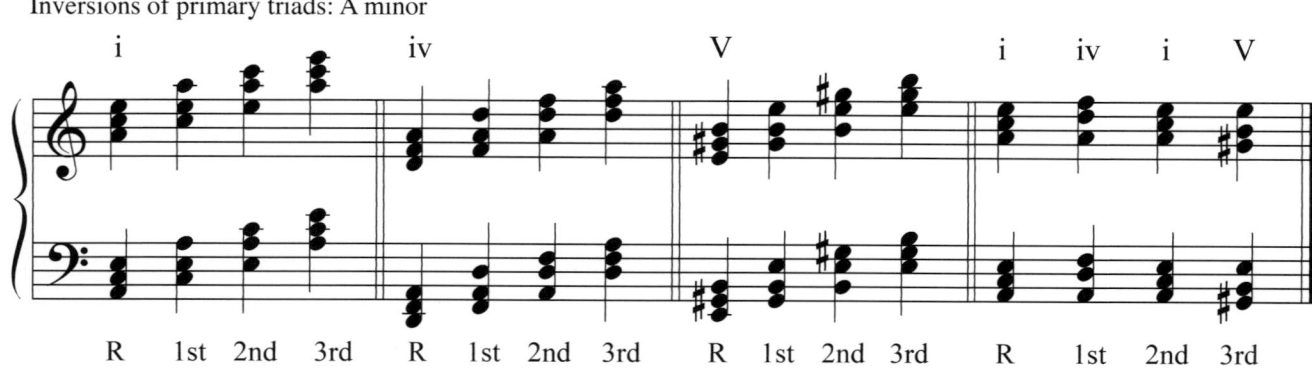

Appendix 1: Triads/inversions cont'd

Root position triads: F Major

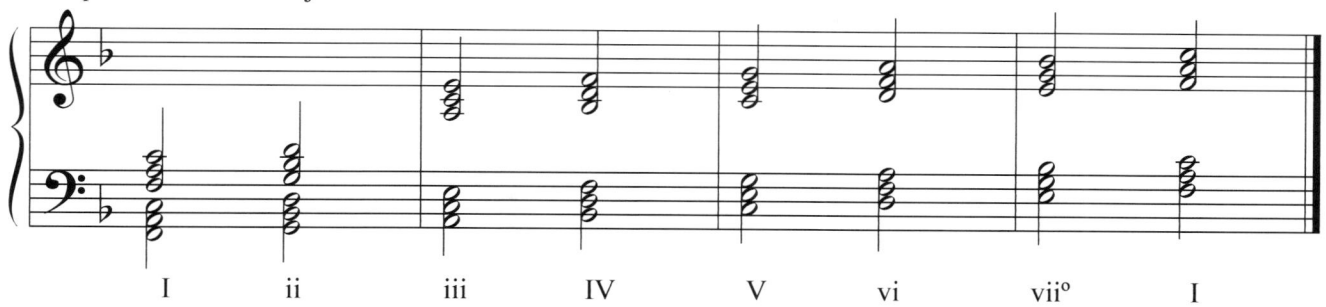

Inversions of primary triads: F Major

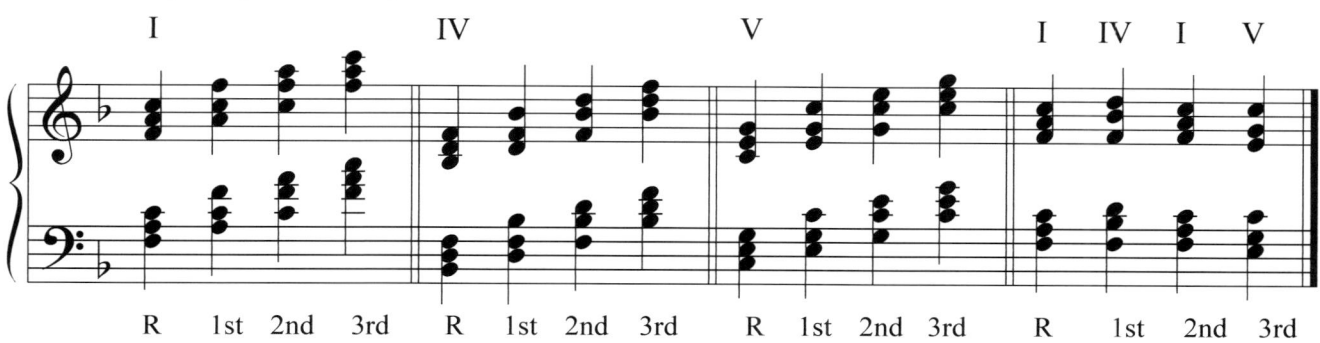

Root position triads: D minor

Inversions of primary triads: D minor

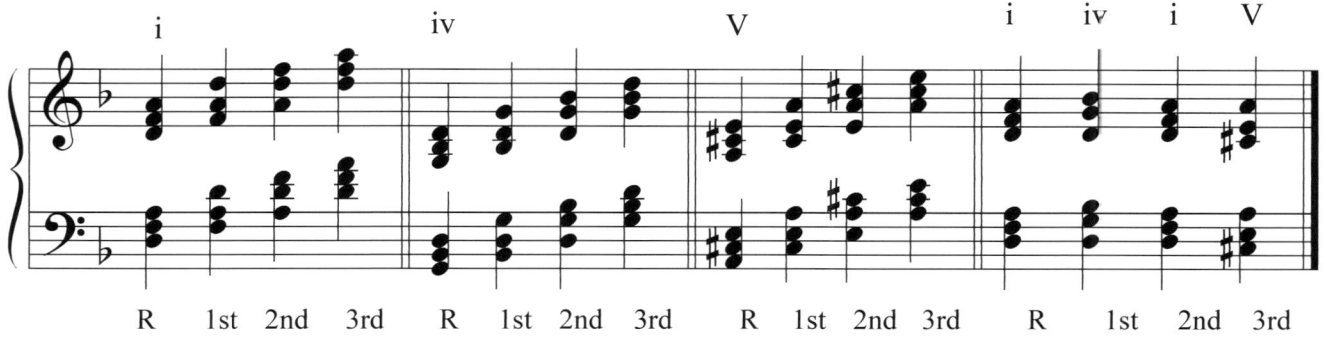

Appendix 1: Triads/inversions cont'd

Root position triads: G Major

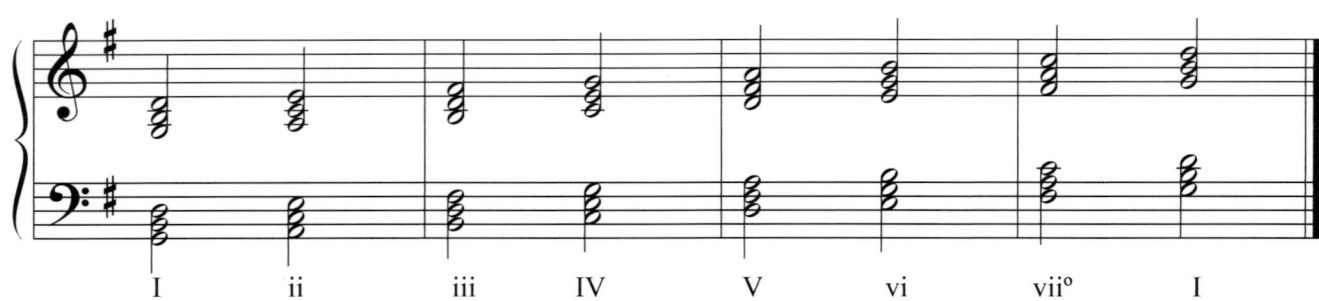

Inversions of primary triads: G Major

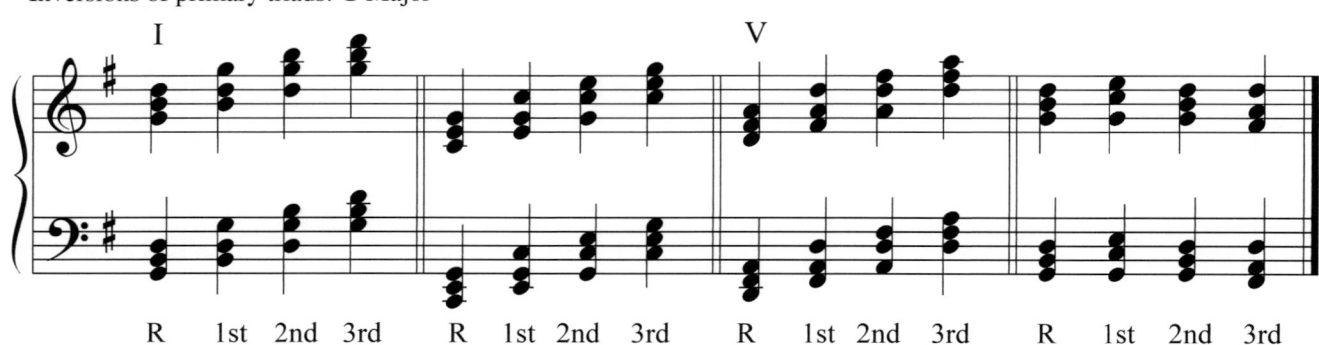

Root position triads: E minor

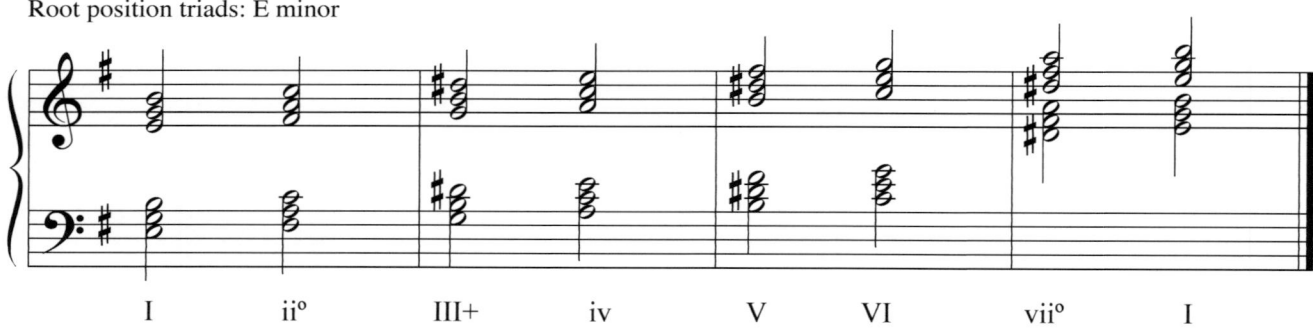

Inversions of primary triads: E minor

Appendix 1: Triads/inversions cont'd

Root position triads: D Major

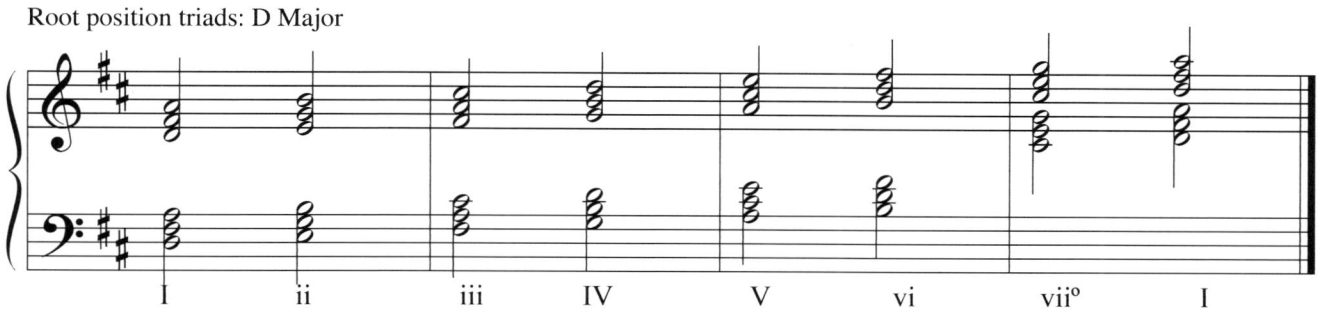

Inversions of primary triads: D Major

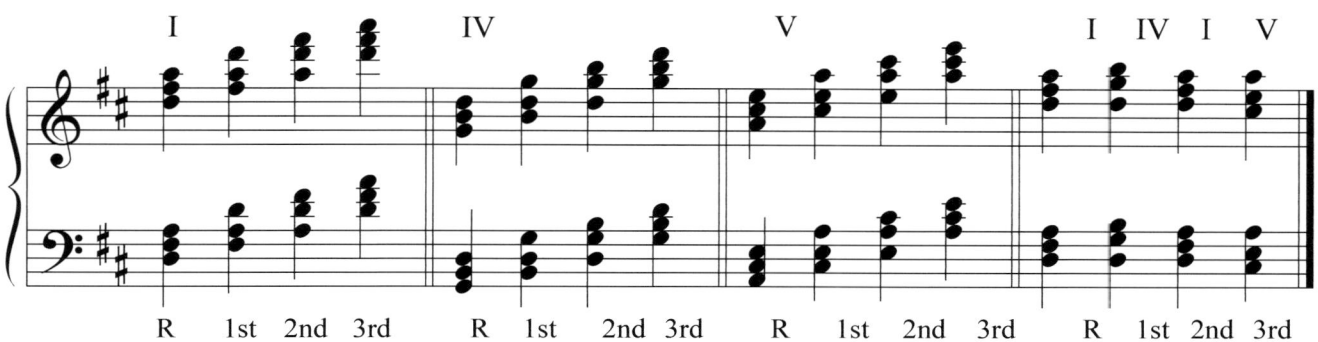

Root position triads: B minor

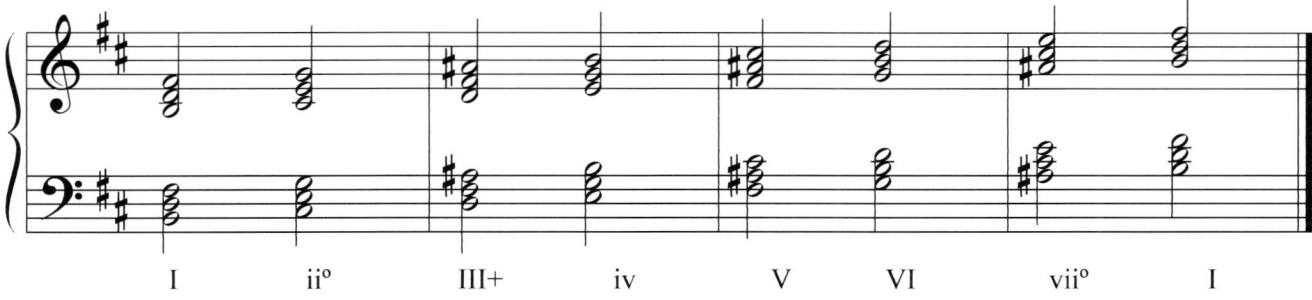

Inversions of primary triads: B minor

Appendix 1: Triads/inversions cont'd

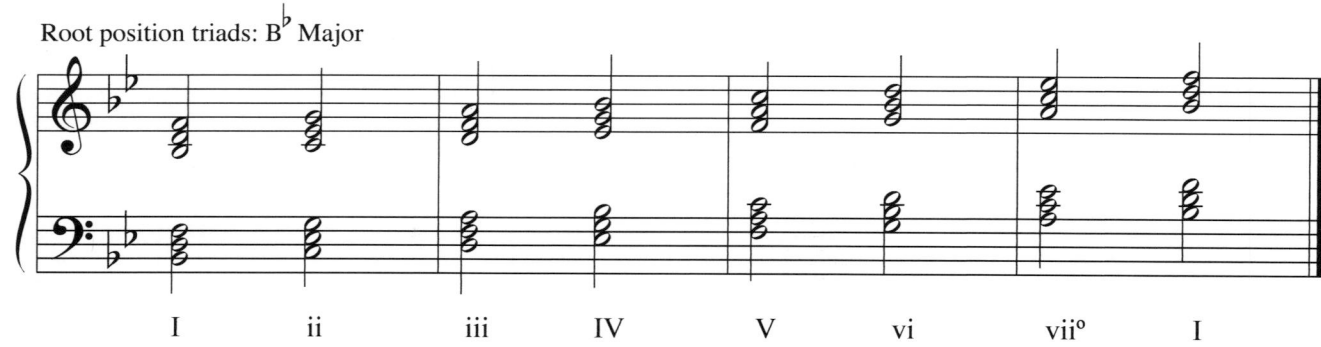

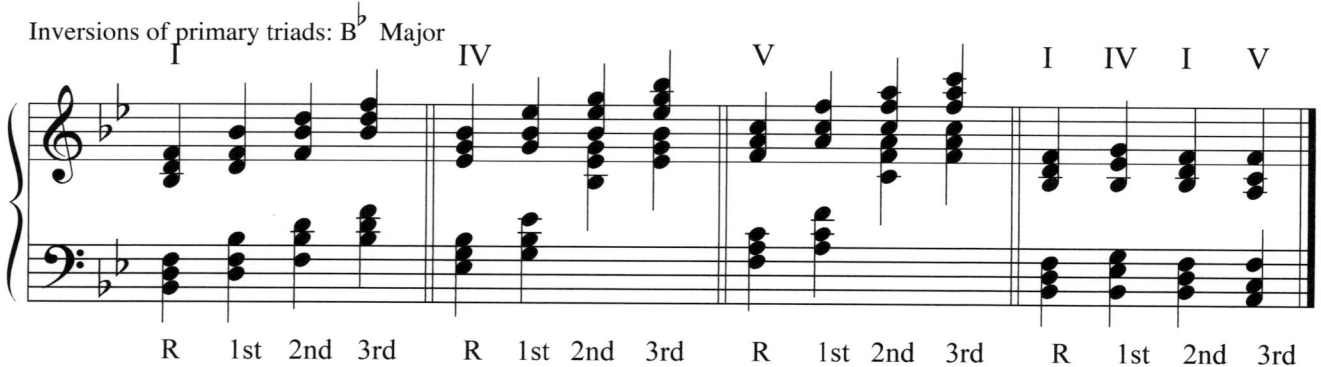

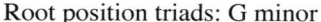

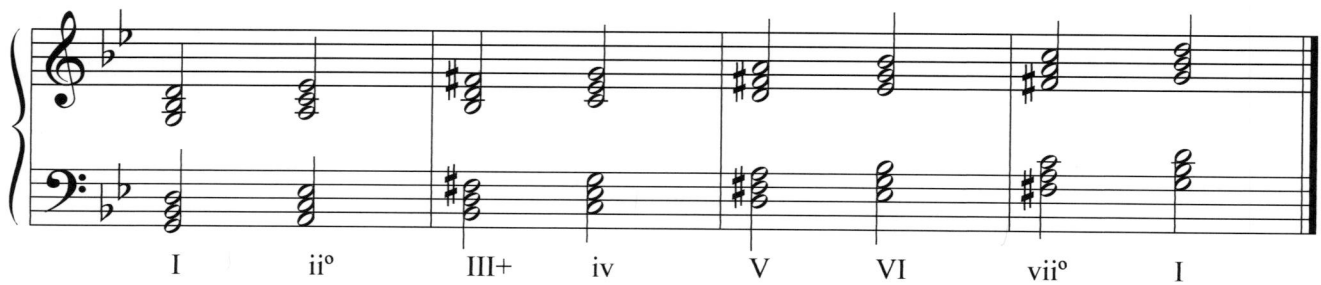

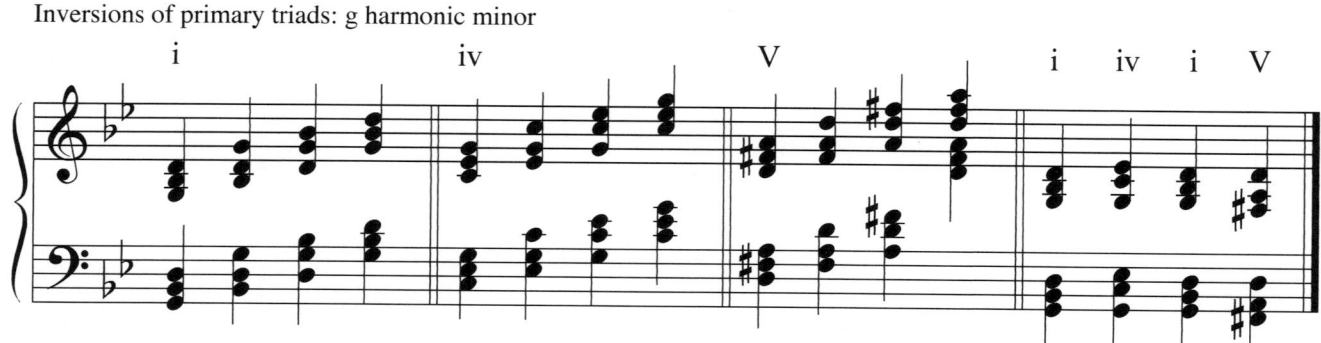

Appendix 2: Melodic Phrases

The material presented here is intended to supplement the harmonized melody and improvisation examples. "Melodic phrase" refers to the phrase construction found in simple common melodies such as popular music, folk tunes, hymn tunes and chorales. Although this material may apply to phrase construction found in larger classical music literature, generally the melodic phrase construction of art music is more complex and is beyond the scope of these materials.

Melodies are comprised of PHRASES. For example, the following melody consists of three phrases:

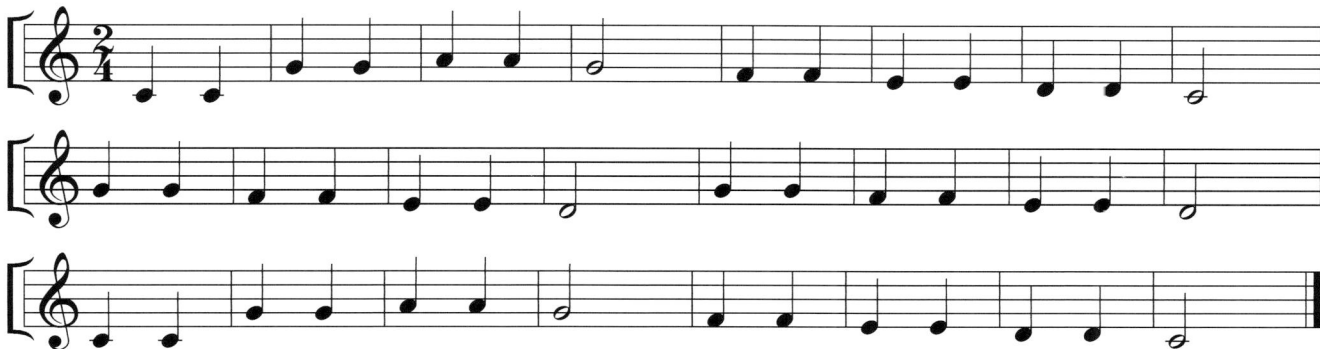

Here is a common definition of PHRASE:

> A phrase is the SHORTest passage of music expressing a COMPLETE MUSICAL THOUGHT and ending in a CADENCE.*

There are three key points to this definition: (1) short, (2) complete musical thought, and (3) cadence. Hopefully, "short" will not need extensive elaboration. However, a common error in determining a phrase is getting it TOO short. More on this later.

COMPLETE MUSICAL THOUGHT means an instance of tension / relaxation. This duality is the basis of "complete musical thought" and is related to the same kind of duality present in classical poetic meters. In the above example, each phrase can easily be divided into its respective tension / relaxation (i.e., each phrase = 4 meas.; tension = 2 meas., relaxation = 2 meas.; half notes indicate points of division). Not all melodies are this obvious. However, a great number of successful melodies do consist of combinations of 4 or 8 measure phrases. With this explanation of "complete musical thought" in mind, examine the above melody again. It is easy to understand why some might make the mistake of defining the phrases in this melody as consisting of 2 measures instead of 4 measures. However, after playing or singing this example the tension / relaxation scenario should become apparent. This particular melody has three phrases and in that regard is not as common as many melodies which have 2 or 4 phrases.

In the above definition, "cadence" does not mean what it meant in an earlier section of this book -- a simple progression of block chords. Instead, CADENCE here means a point of relaxation of the tension at the end of the phrase. There are specific kinds of cadences and all phrases end with one of these specific cadences (see Appendix 3).

Analyze the melodies in the **Melodies for Harmonization** section of this book to determine their phrase construction. In addition to finding tension / relaxation, you might look for these often obvious characteristics of phrase construction:

- Sometimes the CADENCE POINT is the longest note value of the phrase. See section on **Melodies for Harmonization,** examples #7, #23, #26, #29, #31, #35, #39, #42, #43, #46, #47, #48, #53, and #57.

- Usually, phrases consist of 4 or 8 measures (depending on the tempo) as in the example above. This isn't always the case, but the majority of common melodies do have this kind of phrase construction. Check out AMERICA, p. 36. The first phrase has six measures. NOTE: when you are counting measures to determine phrase length, don't count incomplete ("pick-up) measures that may begin a tune ("anacrusis"). See melodies #11 or #17.

* Definition based on Douglass Green's, *Form in Tonal Music*, 2nd edition, Harcourt Brace Jovanovich College Publisher, 1979.

Appendix 3: Melodic Cadences

As mentioned in **Appendix 2**, melodic phrases end with a cadence. In this sense, "cadence" refers to what happens at the end of a phrase and has nothing to do with the "block-chord" cadences (chord progressions) that you are required to learn in order to harmonize melodies and improvise. Here, CADENCE is a "point of rest" at the end of a phrase.

There are only TWO categories of cadences: (1) conclusive, and (2) inconclusive. All types of cadences fall into these two categories. A CONCLUSIVE CADENCE is a cadence on the I chord and an INCONCLUSIVE CADENCE is a cadence on a chord other than the I chord, for example the V chord.

Regarding CONCLUSIVE CADENCES, there are 2 types: (a) authentic, and (b) plagal. An AUTHENTIC CADENCE consists of 2 chords where the PENULTIMATE (next-to-last) chord contains a leading tone. Consequently, the most typical kind of AUTHENTIC CADENCE is V or V7 moving to I. In a PLAGAL CADENCE, the penultimate chord does not have a leading tone. The most typical kind of PLAGAL CADENCE is IV moving to the I chord. In an AUTHENTIC CADENCE, if the I chord is in root position and the tonic is in the melody (top most voice), then it is known as a "perfect authentic cadence."

INCONCLUSIVE CADENCES are not divided into types like conclusive cadences. There is only one type of inconclusive cadence -- those that cadence on a chord other than the I chord, for example the V chord. Another name for the inconclusive cadence is HALF CADENCE. It is important to know that a cadence on V is not the definition of "half cadence" but merely an EXAMPLE of a half cadence. Other half cadences could be cadences on IV ("Auld Lang Syne"), cadences on III ("I've been working on the rail road"), and cadences on vi (deceptive cadence). There is no such thing as a "perfect half cadence." PERFECT when applied to a cadence only refers to an authentic cadence.

To successfully harmonize a melody, it is important to have a step-by-step procedure rather than just willy-nilly sticking in chords. Here is a practical procedure for harmonizing a melody. If you use this you will have consistent success:

1. Identify the phrases. Often phrases can be identified by counting 4 or 8 measures (the majority of common melodies in the western tradition have phrases constructed of 4 or 8 measures), looking for the longest note value (often the cadence point at the end of a phrase is the longest note value of the phrase), or by looking for some aspect of tension and relaxation (question/answer). See the melody below for reference.

2. Harmonize the CADENCE POINTS first. The cadence point is the 2nd chord of the two-chord progression of the cadence, for example V7 - I. The V7 chord is the "penultimate chord" and the I chord is the "cadence point." Generally, there are only two possibilities to harmonize the cadence point: I or V. Remember (from above), there are ONLY TWO categories of cadences: conclusive and non conclusive. So, once you identify the cadence points at the ends of the various phrases it should be relatively easy to determine if the cadence points are I or V. If the cadence point is a V, then it is better to cadence on V rather than V7 (although for Level I piano, the V chord voicing is not presented so it is OK to cadence on V7 rather than V).

3. Next, harmonize the PENULTIMATE CHORD -- that is, the chord right before the cadence point. If the cadence point is the I chord, then you have two possibilities: (a) V7 - I, or (b) IV - I. In the first case that would be an authentic cadence and in the second case it would be a plagal cadence. It most cases it simply doesn't matter which possibility you use. If the cadence point is not a I chord (it's going to be an inconclusive cadence), then your 1st choice should be the V chord since BY FAR this is the most common inconclusive (half) cadence. Yes, there are rare example where a IV chord or a III chord would work, but your BEST CHOICE would simply be to use the V chord. Do not cadence on a ii chord. If you feel the chord HAS to be the ii chord, then chances are you are trying to harmonize the "tension" part of the phrase (as in, tension/relaxation) and you have not really found the true cadence point of the phrase.

4. Harmonize the rest of the melody. Now that you have the cadences at the ends of the phrases harmonized, go ahead and harmonize the rest of the melody using the suggested harmonic rhythm. From here on out, the harmonization procedure will be relative straight forward: if the melody note is in the chord you are trying to use, then IT WILL WORK. There are some simple guidelines to use: (a) often the melody notes will outline specific chords and this will be a good

Material based on Douglass Green's, *Form in Tonal Music*, 2nd edition, Harcourt Brace Jovanovich College Publisher, 1979.

clue as to what chord to use, (b) it's OK to use the same chord consecutively -- you don't have to change chords on every instances of the harmonic rhythm, (c) V7-I used within the phrase works best when the I chord is on a strong beat and the V7 chord is on a weak beat. This is not a hard and fast rule, but it generally works well.

Here is an example:

Find the phrases, identify and then harmonize the cadence points. How many phrases does this tune have?

-- The answer is TWO PHRASES. Count 8 measure phrases and look for the LONGEST note values.
-- The longest note values ARE the CADENCE POINTS, and you should be able to see that there are 2 phrases.
-- There is an aspect of TENSION from the beginning through the 2nd beat of meas. 4. This is followed by a RELAXATION from the 3rd beat of meas. 4 through the cadence point of meas. 7 and 8. A similar structure can be found from the 3rd beat of meas. 9 through the 2nd cadence point at the end of the tune.
-- The first cadence point should be harmonized by the V chord (or V7, if Level Preparatory or Level I).
-- The second cadence point should be harmonized by the I chord.

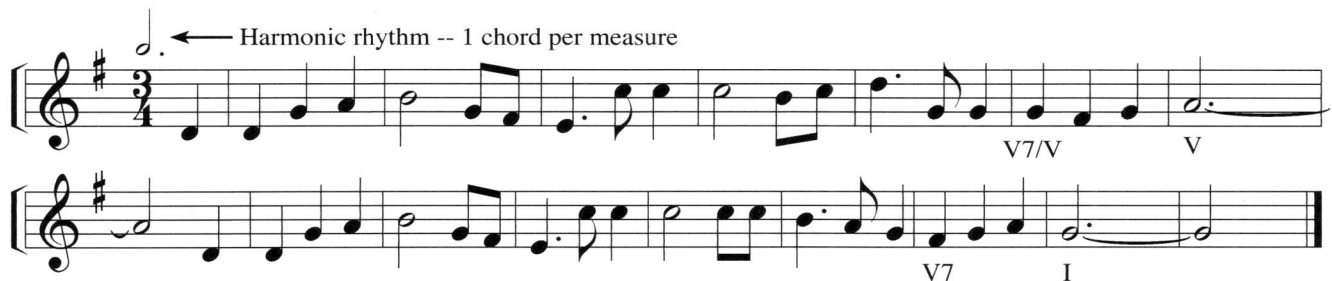

-- The 1st cadence is an inconclusive cadence (half cadence); the second cadence is a conclusive (authentic) cadence.

Continue harmonizing the rest of the tune. Keep it SIMPLE. It's OK to use the same chord consecutively, especially if the melody outlines specific chords. Keep in mind the HARMONIC RHYTHM, in this case -- one dotted half note for each measure. Notice how the first phrase cadences on a V chord and then moves to a V7 chord. This creates a stronger cadence than just cadencing on the V7 chord. Although, for Preparatory and Level I piano this will not be an option.

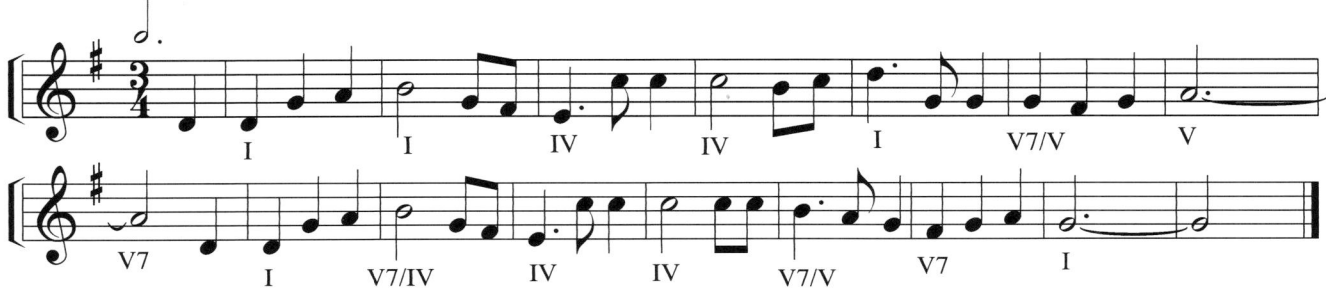

Notice how the V7/V chord is used at the cadence at the end of the 1st phrase (meas. 7). This is one of the most obvious uses of the V7/V chord -- right before the V chord at a HALF CADENCE.

Appendix 4: Non-Chord Tones

A NON-CHORD TONE is a note in a melody which is not part of the chord or harmony which is being used for harmonization at the point where the NON-CHORD TONE appears. Generally, there are two types of NON-CHORD TONES:

1. Unaccented (occurs on a weak beat or a weak part of a beat)
2. Accented (occurs on a strong beat)

The terms "accented" and "unaccented" are subjective because the "feel" of accented/unaccented depends on such factors as tempo and harmonic rhythm.

Here are some examples of NON-CHORD TONES. The numbers indicate different NON-CHORD TONES which are explained below:

1. PASSING TONE. One of the most common non-chord tones, the PASSING TONE "passes" between two adjacent chord tones. "Adjacent" means the next chord tone, either up or down. In the chord, C-E-G, "E" and "G" are adjacent but "C" and "G" are nonadjacent. So the PASSING TONE between C-E would be "D". The PASSING TONE between E-G would be F.

2. NEIGHBOR TONE. Also one of the most common-chord tones, the NEIGHBOR TONE is a diatonic step UP or DOWN from any chord tone. If the NEIGHBOR TONE is above the chord-tone then it's an "UPPER NEIGHBOR TONE." And if it's below, its called a LOWER NEIGHBOR TONE. The example above (#2) is a LOWER NEIGHBOR TONE.

3. ACCENTED PASSING TONE. If a passing tone occurs on a strong beat then it's called an ACCENTED PASSING TONE. Notice that the note before and after are chord-tones.

4. ANTICIPATION. An ANTICIPATION, "anticipates" the upcoming chord. So, this implies that at least TWO chords and 3 melody notes are involved. The 1st note is a chord tone associated with the 1st chord and the 2nd note (which is the actual ANTICIPATION) is a non-chord tone associated with the 2nd chord. In the example above (#4), the "E" is a chord-tone and is associated with the C major triad on beat 1. The "F" on beat 2 is not part of the C major triad but is a part of the F major triad on beat 3. An ANTICIPATION always occurs on a weak beat.

5. SUSPENSION. A SUSPENSION is the similar to an ANTICIPATION except that it always occurs on a STRONG beat. It must have TWO chords involved and THREE melody notes. The 1st melody note is associated with the 1st chord and occurs on a WEAK beat. The 2nd melody note is THE SAME as the 1st melody note but is associated with the second chord and occurs on a strong beat. This 2nd melody note is the actual SUSPENSION and it's a NON-CHORD TONE (not part of the 2nd chord). The 3rd melody note "resolves" to a chord tone in the 2nd chord.

6. APPOGGIATURA. An APPOGGIATURA is a type of ACCENTED non-chord tone and is very similar to a SUSPENSION: it must have TWO chords involved and THREE melody notes. Here's the difference: the 2nd melody note is DIFFERENT from the 1st melody note and it SKIPS to a non-chord tone associated with the 2nd chord and then "resolves" BY STEP in the OPPOSITE DIRECTION from the skip. If this seems complex, then just study the example. Some music theorists consider all ACCENTED non-chord tones to be APPOGGIATURAS. See "appoggiatura" in *Harvard's Dictionary of Music*.

7. ESCAPE TONE. An ESCAPE TONE occurs on a WEAK beat and consists of a step (either up or down) followed by a skip in the opposite direction to a CHORD TONE in either the same chord or a different chord.

There are other NON-CHORD TONES but they will not be discussed here. You will no doubt cover them in your theory courses.

A question that is often asked by beginning theory students is, "Good grief! Why does all this matter?" Here's a simple answer:

Music theory is the SCIENCE of music. In any scientific field, one endeavors is to CLASSIFY all possible phenomena. For example, in the field of geology, one endeavors to classify all rocks and all phenomena concerning rocks. The same is true in ornithology, entomology, astronomy, physics, etc. The study of music is no different. To UNDERSTAND music at a deep level, one has to classify and NAME all possible musical phenomena. Although this may seem tedious and unimportant to the novice, it is invaluable to the professional musician.

Weekly Assignment Schedule

Week 1: Welcome to class
    Prepare to take a written quiz <u>next class period</u> on all scale groups (pp. 112 - 113), <u>written material only</u>. The quiz will cover:
      1. What scales are in each group?
      2. What are the characteristics of the scales in each group?
      3. Major and minor key signatures

    In addition:
- Explore the Sequencer Controls for Level 4 Piano.
- You will be required to play two memorized repertory pieces as part of your Piano Proficiency Examination. Choose two repertory pieces from this book and commit to those for the remainder of the semester. Your first repertory piece is due on Week 4 (with the music) and your second repertory piece is due on Week 5 (with the music). So, begin practicing those pieces immediately.

Week 2: Scales; Cadences; Harmonized Melodies; Transposition; Exercises
- Scales: Group 3 major Scales: B-flat; E-flat; A-flat, pp. 113; 121
- Cadence: Cadence #3, p. 56 in all major keys
- Harmonized melodies:
  - Study the **Procedures for Harmonized Melodies**, p. 58 - 59
  - Be prepared to take a written quiz on these procedures.
  - Harmonize melody # 42, p. 69 (*Apres de ma blonde*)
- Transposition: Transpose each part separately for example # 16, p. 86 up and down a whole step AND up and down a half step.
- Exercises: Exercises 1 - 3, pp. 130 - 135

Week 3: Scales; Triads; Establish a Key; Patriotic Song/Hymn; Sight Reading; Exercises
- Sight Reading: Practice sight reading examples, pp. 82 - 93
- Scales: Group 3 minor Scales: C-sharp minor; F-sharp minor; A-flat (G-sharp) minor. pp. 113; 121 - 122
- Triads: All major triads, pp. 48-49
- Establish Keys: major keys on the white notes of the piano. Use the chord progression for Cadence #1 on p. 54.
- Patriotic Song/Hymn: Play your patriotic song or hymn using the music. Minimum -- hands separate.
- Exercises: Exercises 1 - 3, pp. 130 - 135

Week 4: Repertory; Repertory, Scales; Cadences; Improvisation; Sight Reading; Exercises
- Sight Reading: Practice sight reading examples, pp. 82 - 95
- Repertory: Play your FIRST repertory piece with the music: slowly and with a steady tempo
- Scales: All Group 3 Scales, pp. 113; 121 - 122
- Cadence: Cadence #3, p. 56 in all major keys
- Improvisation: Review the Improvisation Procedures pp. 74-79
  - Be prepared to take a written quiz on these procedures
  - Write out rhythmic motives on p. 76
  - Do Improvisations #1, p. 80 using rhythmic motives you made up using Cadence #3, p. 56. This is a REVIEW from last semester.
- Exercises: Exercises 1 - 3, pp. 130 - 135

Week 5: Repertory; Scales; Improvisation; Sight Reading; Exercises
- Sight Reading: Practice sight reading examples, pp. 82 - 95
- Repertory: Play your SECOND repertory piece with the music: slowly and with a steady tempo
- Scales: Review all Group 1 major Scales, pp. 112; 114
- Improvisation: Continue to review pp. 74-79. Work out the melody of "Happy Birthday" in F Maj. & G Maj.
- Exercises: Exercises 1 - 4, pp. 138 - 145

Week 6: Scales; Cadences; Harmonized Melodies; Transposition; Improvisation; Sight Reading; Exercises
- Sight Reading: Practice sight reading examples, pp. 82 - 95
- Scales: Review all Group 1 harmonic minor Scales, pp. 112; 116
- Cadences: Review Cadence #4 all major keys, p. 57
- Harmonized Melodies: Harmonize melody #46, p. 70 (*East Side West Side*)
- Transposition: Transpose each part separately for example # 20, p. 88 up and down a whole step AND up and down a half step.
- Do Improvisations #3, p. 81 using rhythmic motives you made up on p. 76..
- Exercises: Exercises 1 - 3, pp. 130 - 135

Week 7: Scales; Triads; Establish a Key; Improvisation; Patriotic Song/Hymn; Sight Reading; Exercises
- Sight Reading: Practice sight reading examples, pp. 82 - 95
- Scales: Review all Group 1 Scales, pp. 112; - 114-116
- Triads: All minor triads, pp. 48-49
- Establish Keys: major keys on the black notes of the piano. Use the chord progression for Cadence #1 on p. 54
- Add primary chords from Cadence #1 to "Happy Birthday" in F Maj. & G Maj. that you worked out from week 5.
- Patriotic Song/Hymn: Play your patriotic song or hymn using the music. Minimum -- hands separate; hands together through the 1st phrase.
- Exercises: Exercises 1 - 3, pp. 130 - 135

Week 8: Scales; Cadences; Harmonized Melodies; Transposition; Improvisation; Sight Reading; Exercises
- Sight Reading: Practice sight reading examples, pp. 82 - 95
- Scales: Review all Group 2 major Scales, p. 112; 117
- Cadences: Review Cadence #4 all minor keys, p. 57
- Harmonized Melodies: Harmonize melody #50, p. 71 (*Carcassi*)
- Transposition: Transpose each part separately for example # 38, p. 94 up and down a whole step AND up and down a half step.
- Improvisation: Continue to review pp. 74-79. Do Improvisations #2, p. 81 using rhythmic motives you made up on p. 76.
- Exercises: Exercises 1 - 4, pp. 130 - 137

Week 9: Scales; Improvisation; Triads; Establish a Key; Transposition; Patriotic Song/Hymn; Sight Reading; Exercises
- Sight Reading: Practice sight reading examples, pp. 82 - 95
- Scales: Review all Group 2 harmonic and melodic minor Scales, p. 112; 119-120
- Add V7/IV from Cadence #4 to "Happy Birthday" in F Maj. & G Maj. that you worked out from week 7.
- Triads: All Augmented triads, pp. 50-51
- Establish Keys: minor keys on the white notes of the piano. Use the chord progression for Cadence #1 on p. 54
- Patriotic Song/Hymn: Play your patriotic song or hymn using the music. Minimum -- hands separate; hands together through the 2nd phrase.
- Exercises: Exercises 1 - 4, pp. 130 - 137

Week 10: Repertory; Scales; Cadences; Harmonized Melodies; Improvisation; Sight Reading; Exercises
- Sight Reading: Practice sight reading examples, pp. 82 - 95
- Repertory: Play your 1st repertory piece with the music: observe articulation and expression markings
- Scales: Review all Group 2 Scales (major, harmonic minor, melodic minor), pp. 112; 117-120
- Cadences: Review Cadence #3 and Cadence #4 in all required major keys: C, D, F, G, B-flat, pp. 56-57
- Harmonized Melodies: Harmonize melody #43, p. 69 (*Carpenter*)
- Improvisation: Continue to review pp. 74-79. Do Improvisations #3, p. 81 using rhythmic motives you made up on p. 76.
- Exercises: Exercises 1 - 4, pp. 130 - 137

Week 11: Repertory; Scales; Cadences; Harmonization; Improvisation; Sight Reading; Exercises
- Sight Reading: Practice sight reading examples, pp. 82 - 95
- Repertory: Play your 2nd repertory piece with the music: observe articulation and expression markings
- Scales: Review all Group 3 Scales, pp. 113; 112-122
- Cadences: Review Cadence #2 and Cadence #4 in minor keys: Am; Dm; Em; Gm; B-flat m, pp. 56 - 57
- Harmonization: Harmonize melody #42, p. 75 (*Ash Grove*)
- Improvisation: Continue to review pp. 74-79. Do Improvisations #4, p. 80 using rhythmic motives you made up on p. 76.
- Exercises: Exercises 1 - 4, pp. 130 - 137

Week 12: Scales; Improvisation; Triads; Establish a Key; Patriotic Song/Hymn; Sight Reading; Exercises
- Sight Reading: Practice sight reading examples, pp. 82 - 95
- Scales: Play all required Scales, pp. 112 - 122
- Add V7/V from Cadence #4 to "Happy Birthday" in F Maj. & G Maj. that you worked out from week 9.
- Transposition: Practice transposing single lines (treble clef or bass clef), pp. 27 - 90
- Triads: All diminished triads, pp. 50-51
- Establish Keys: minor keys on the black notes of the piano. Use the chord progression for Cadence #1 on p. 54
- Patriotic Song/Hymn: Play your patriotic song or hymn using the music
- Exercises: Exercises 1 - 4, pp. 130 - 137

Week 13: Repertory; Scales; Cadences; Harmonization; Improvisation; Transposition; Triads; Establish a Key; Patriotic song/Hymn; Sight Reading; Exercises
- Sight Reading: Practice sight reading examples, pp. 82 - 95
- Repertory: Play your 1st repertory piece from memory
- Scales: Play all required Scales, pp. 112 - 122
- Cadences: All Cadences to date: Cadence #2 (maj/min); Cadence #3 (maj); Cadence #4 (maj/min), pp. 55 - 57
- Harmonization: Practice harmonizing melodies, pp. 67 - 73
- Improvisation: Practice improvising on any of the chord progressions, pp. 80 - 81
- Transposition: On your own, practice any of the examples, pp. 82-95
- Triads: All Triads (Maj/min/Aug/dim), pp. 48-51
- Establish Keys: all major and minor keys. Use the chord progression for Cadence #1 on p. 54
- Patriotic Song/Hymn: Play your patriotic song or hymn using the music
- Exercises: Exercises 1 - 4, pp. 130 - 137

Week 14: Repertory; Scales; Cadences; Harmonization; Improvisation; Transposition; Triads; Establish a Key; Patriotic song/Hymn; Sight Reading; Exercises
- Sight Reading: Practice sight reading examples, pp. 82 - 95
- Repertory: Play your 2nd repertory piece from memory
- Scales: Play all required Scales, pp. 112 - 122
- Cadences: All Cadences to date: Cadence #2 (maj/min); Cadence #3 (maj); Cadence #4 (maj/min), pp. 55 - 57
- Harmonization: Practice harmonizing melodies, pp. 67 - 73
- Improvisation: Practice improvising on any of the chord progressions, pp. 80 - 81
- Transposition: On your own, practice any of the examples, pp. 82-95
- Triads: All Triads (Maj/min/Aug/dim), pp. 48-51
- Establish Keys: all major and minor keys. Use the chord progression for Cadence #1 on p. 54
- Patriotic Song/Hymn: Play your patriotic song or hymn using the music
- Exercises: Exercises 1 - 4, pp. 130 - 137

Week 15: Repertory; Scales; Cadences; Harmonization; Improvisation; Transposition; Triads; Establish a Key; Patriotic song/ Hymn; Sight Reading; Exercises
- Sight Reading: Practice sight reading examples, pp. 82 - 95
- Repertory: Play both repertory pieces from memory
- Have all the following material prepared. Your instructor may hear any of it for this week's assignment:

- All required Scales, pp. 112 - 122
- All Cadences to date: Cadence #2 (maj/min); Cadence #3 (maj); Cadence #4 (maj/min), pp. 55 - 57
- All Triads (Maj/min/Aug/dim), pp. 48-51
- Practice harmonizing melodies from pp. 67-73, but be prepared to play any ONE of your choice.
- Practice improvising on any of the chord progressions, pp. 80 - 81
- Practice transposing any of the examples, pp. 82-95
- Patriotic Song/Hymn: Play your patriotic song or hymn using the music
- Establish Keys: all major and minor keys. Use the chord progression for Cadence #1 on p. 54
- Exercises 1 - 4, pp. 130 - 137

Final Exam:

A Final Exam will be arranged by your Instructor for the regularly scheduled exam time for this coarse (see printed or ONLINE Final Exam schedule). The Final Exam will consist of the following specific material required for the Piano Proficiency Examination:

- Scales
- Sight Read a simple piece (to be provided to the instructor by the coordinator)
- Play root-position triads on any note
- Establish a key in selected keys

(See following page for more information on the Piano Proficiency Examination.)

In addition, your Instructor may hear any other material (to be announced) to determine a Final Exam Grade for this course.

Class Notes

Level Four Assignments

Wk. #	Scales	Repertory	Cadences	Harm. Mel.	Improv.*	Transpose**	Triads*	Establish a Key	Pat/Hymns	Exercises
1	Quiz on all scales -- written material only. See pages 112 - 113.									
2	Group III Majors		#3, p. 56, All Major keys	#42, p. 69 *Apres de ma...*		#16, p. 86*				#1, 2, 3 pp. 130-135
3	Group III Minors						All Major Triads pp. 48-49	Cadence #1, p. 54 Major keys on the white notes	Your requirement	#1, 2, 3 pp. 130-135
4	All Group III	1st Repertory Piece with the music	#3, p. 56, All Major keys		Review pp. 74-79 Do #1, p. 80 See detail, p. 154					#1, 2, 3 pp. 130-135
5	Group I Majors	2nd Repertory Piece with the music			Play the melody to "Happy Birthday" in F Maj & G Maj.					#1, 2, 3 pp. 130-135
6	Group I Minors		#4, p. 57, All Major keys	#46, p. 70 *East Side...*	#3, pg. 81	#20, p. 88*				#1, 2, 3 pp. 130-135
7	All Group I				Add primary chords to "Happy Birthday" in F Maj & G Maj. using Cadence #1.		All Minor Triads pp. 48-49	Cadence #1, p. 54 Major keys on the black notes	Your requirement	#1, 2, 3 pp. 130-135
8	Group II Majors		#4, p. 57, All Minor keys	#50, p. 71 *Carcassi*	#2, pg. 81	#38, p. 94*				#1, 2, 3, 4 pp. 130-137
9	Group II Minors				Add V7/IV to "Happy Birthday" in F Maj & G Maj. using Cadence #4.		All Augmented Triads pp. 50-51	Cadence #1, p. 54 Minor keys on the white notes	Your requirement	#1, 2, 3, 4 pp. 130-137
10	All Group II	1st Repertory Piece with the music	#3 & #4, pp. 56-57 All Major keys	#43, p. 69 *Carpenter*	#3, pg. 81					#1, 2, 3, 4 pp. 130-137
11	All Gr. III again	2nd Repertory Piece with the music	# 2 & #4, pp. 55; 57 All Minor keys		#4, pg. 80					#1, 2, 3, 4 pp. 130-137
12	ALL Scales				Add V7/V to "Happy Birthday" in F Maj & G Maj. using Cadence #4.	#27, p. 90*	All Diminished Triads pp. 50-51	Cadence #1, p. 54 Minor keys on the black notes	Your requirement	#1, 2, 3, 4 pp. 130-137
13	ALL Scales	1st Repertory Piece from memory	All Cadences to date	Practice harmonizing melodies on your own: pp. 67-73	Practice improvisations on your own: pp. 80-81	Practice transpositions on your own: pp. 82-95*	All Triads pp. 50-51	Cadence #1, p. 54 All Major and Minor keys	Your requirement	#1, 2, 3, 4 pp. 130-137
14	ALL Scales	2nd Repertory Piece from memory	All Cadences to date	Practice harmonizing melodies on your own: pp. 67-73	Practice improvisations on your own: pp. 80-81	Practice transpositions on your own: pp. 82-95*	All Triads pp. 50 51	Cadence #1, p. 54 All Major and Minor keys	Your requirement	#1, 2, 3, 4 pp. 130-137
15	ALL Scales	Both rep. pieces from memory	All Cadences to date	Practice harmonizing melodies on your own: pp. 67-73	Practice improvisations on your on: p. 80-81	Practice transpositions on your own: pp. 82-95*	All Triads pp. 50-51	Cadence #1, p. 54 All Major and Minor keys	Your requirement	#1, 2, 3, 4 pp. 130-137

All scales,, cadences, triads, and exercises should be performed from memory when playing for a grade. Failure to do so will result in a lowered grade.

* Some assignments will have more detailed information in the Assignment Schedule section located on pp. 154-157.

** Sudents are only required to play **TRANSPOSITIONS** one part at a time; however, both parts should be prepared up and down a whole step AND up and down a half step.